KENTUCKY

DAILY
DEVOTIONS
FOR
DIE-HARD
FANS

WILDCATS

KENTUCKY

WILDCATS

Daily Devotions for Die-Hard Fans

ACC
Clemson Tigers
Duke Blue Devils
FSU Seminoles
Georgia Tech Yellow Jackets
North Carolina Tar Heels
NC State Wolfpack
Virginia Cavaliers
Virginia Tech Hokies

BIG 10
Michigan Wolverines
Ohio State Buckeyes
Penn State Nittany Lions

BIG 12
Baylor Bears
Oklahoma Sooners
Oklahoma State Cowboys
TCU Horned Frogs
Texas Longhorns
Texas Tech Red Raiders

SEC
Alabama Crimson Tide
Arkansas Razorbacks
Auburn Tigers
More Auburn Tigers
Florida Gators
Georgia Bulldogs
More Georgia Bulldogs
Kentucky Wildcats
LSU Tigers
Mississippi State Bulldogs
Missouri Tigers
Ole Miss Rebels
South Carolina Gamecocks
More South Carolina Gamecocks
Texas A&M Aggies
Tennessee Volunteers

NASCAR

KENTUCKY

DAILY
DEVOTIONS
FOR
DIE-HARD
FANS

WILDCATS

IN THE BEGINNING

Read Genesis 1, 2:1-3.

"God saw all that he had made, and it was very good" (v. 1:31).

The players sometimes wore football pads, they had to buy the team's only ball, and they didn't have a coach. It was the beginning, however, of Kentucky basketball.

The school then known as Kentucky State College played its first men's intercollegiate basketball game on Feb. 6, 1903. As was typical in the sport's early days, that first squad was mostly football players trying to stay in shape during the winter.

As a result, the game was pretty much indoor football. Reflecting the sport's physical nature, the Transylvania team showed up for a game with State in 1907 wearing football pads. Thomas Bryant, who played from 1905-07, said of the early games, "A good fight was the expected thing."

Basketball at UK began "on a shoestring." The team had only one basketball, which was bought by the players. They chipped in quarters or half-dollars to raise the three dollars required to buy "the heavy little balloon." That one ball was used for both practices and games. As Bryant noted, "If something had happened to that ball, we couldn't have played."

The team had no coach. The players practiced on their own, and the responsibilities were handled by a student manager. W.B. Wendt, who was the manager in 1906, remarked that he was "a one-man operation. I made the schedule, printed the tickets, collected money, paid the bills, was in charge of the team on the road, and sometimes swept the floor."

That first game was against Georgetown College, which had been playing for months. The results showed it. The Baptists led 7-1 at the half, and as the *Lexington Herald* reported, "During the latter part of the game, State College weakened appreciably." The feisty but outmatched State boys lost 15-6.

Twelve days later, though, the team made history by edging the Lexington YMCA 11-10 for the school's first-ever win.

Beginnings are important, but what we make of them is even more important. Consider, for example, how far the UK basketball program has come since that first season. Every morning, you get a gift from God: a new beginning. God hands to you as an expression of divine love a new day full of promise and the chance to right the wrongs in your life. You can use the day to pay a debt, start a new relationship, replace a burned-out light bulb, tell your family you love them, chase a dream, solve a nagging problem . . . or not.

God simply provides the gift. How you use it is up to you. People often talk wistfully about starting over or making a new beginning. God gives you the chance with the dawning of every new day. You have the chance today to make things right — and that includes your relationship with God.

We didn't play for championships but for bloody noses.
— Early UK basketball player Thomas Bryant

Every day is not just a dawn
but a precious chance to start over or begin anew.

ON CALL

Read 1 Samuel 3:1-18.

"The Lord came and stood there, calling as at the other times, 'Samuel! Samuel!' Then Samuel said, 'Speak, for your servant is listening'" (v. 10).

Jojo Kemp answered the call, and the Wildcats had the biggest win of the Mark Stoops era to that time.

Kemp was the leading rusher for the 2013 team as a freshman, but he spent much of the early part of the 2014 season as a backup. In the Vanderbilt game, for instance, he saw action only late in the game to help the Cats run out the clock for the 17-7 win.

The following week, Oct. 4, against South Carolina was more of the same. As the game wore on, Kemp had one carry. That single carry was a nice one, a 3-yard run out of the Wildcat formation for Kentucky's first touchdown with 9:15 to go in the second quarter. After that, nothing. But he didn't sulk; instead, he cheered on his teammates and waited for the call. It came in the fourth quarter.

Maybe it came too late. The Gamecocks had apparently taken control of the game with a 38-24 lead in the fourth quarter. When Kemp answered the call, though, they couldn't stop him. Running out of the Wildcat again, he took the direct snap and led the Cats on two scoring drives.

The first covered 47 yards with Kemp carrying the ball on six of the seven snaps. He scored from the 1 with 8:06 left. After the defense forced a punt, the Cats called on Kemp again. This drive covered 75 yards with Kemp carrying the mail on five of the seven plays. At one point, the exhausted runner signaled the sideline that he needed a breather. The coaches told him to stay in and finish what he had started. He did just that, scoring from the 5 with 2:46 left to tie the game and complete the comeback.

After senior linebacker Alvin "Bud" Dupree took an interception back for a touchdown, it was only fitting that Kemp get the call one more time. With three carries, he ran out the clock for the 45-38 win.

A team player is someone who does whatever the coach calls upon him to do for the good of the team. Something quite similar occurs when God places a specific call upon a Christian's life. This is much scarier, though, than putting your team on your back late in the game as Jojo Kemp did against South Carolina.

To many folks, answering God's call means going into the ministry, packing the family up, and moving halfway around the world to some place where folks have never heard of air conditioning, fried chicken, paved roads, or the Kentucky Wildcats. Zambia. The Philippines. Cleveland even.

Not for you, no thank you. And who can blame you?

But God usually calls folks to serve him where they are. In fact, God put you where you are right now, and he has a purpose in placing you there. Wherever you are, you are called to serve him.

When my name was called, I had to go out there and make the best of my opportunity.
                                        — Jojo Kemp on answering the call

**God calls you to serve him right now right where
he has put you, wherever that is.**

SUPERSTITION

Read 1 Samuel 28:3-20.

"Saul then said to his attendants, 'Find me a woman who is a medium, so I may go and inquire of her'" (v. 7).

One of the profession's most superstitious coaches declared he had learned it was bad luck to be superstitious.

Adolph Rupp is, of course, a Kentucky and college basketball legend. During the forty-two seasons from 1930-72 he was head coach at UK, his teams won 876 games, which, at the time, made him the winningest college basketball coach in history.

Rupp was always a media favorite, the press taking special delight in his fascinating and apparently endless superstitions.

For instance, he always carried a buckeye in his pocket. He never varied his routine, running practices the same way and always sitting in the same place on the bus. Before a game and at halftime, he would always hang his coat in the first locker and would wash his hands before he appeared to the team. He never walked onto the court until the UK fight song had been played.

For Rupp, black cats were good news. In his first season at UK, he spotted a black cat before a game and shouted to his players, "Boys, it's in the bag!" He then proceeded to follow the cat's exact path. The Cats won the game.

Rupp was careful to step on the same manhole cover outside Memorial Coliseum before every game -- but always with his right foot. His team manager had to hold up three varieties of chewing gum before a game, and he always chose the one in the middle. He was constantly looking for pennies or hairpins; on game day team managers would secretly strew these good-luck charms in his path so he would feel lucky by game time.

Rupp's most notorious superstition, however, was his brown suit. All forty-two years at UK, he wore a brown suit, brown tie, brown shoes, and brown socks to every Kentucky game.

Black cats are right pretty little things. A medium is a steak. A key chain with a rabbit's foot wasn't too lucky for the rabbit. And what in the world is a blarney stone? About as superstitious as you get is to say "God bless you" when somebody sneezes.

You look indulgently upon good-luck charms, tarot cards, palm readers, astrology, and the like; they're really just amusing and harmless. So what's the problem? Nothing as long as you conduct yourself with the belief that superstitious objects and rituals — from broken mirrors to your daily horoscope — can't bring about good or bad luck. You aren't willing to let such notions and nonsense rule your life.

The danger of superstition lies in the power it has to lure you into trusting it, thus allowing it a degree of influence over your life. In that case, it subverts God's rightful place.

Whether or not it's superstition, something does rule your life. It should be God — and God alone.

I was thinking if you had those brown socks on.
— Guard Jake Bronston when Rupp asked him what he was thinking of
during a game

Superstitions may not rule your life, but
something does; it should be God and God alone.

KENTUCKY

GOAL ORIENTED

Read 1 Peter 1:3-12.

"For you are receiving the goal of your faith, the salvation of your souls" (v. 9).

My goal is to be the greatest point guard ever." For one transcendent season in Lexington, John Wall achieved his goal.

Wall came to Kentucky in 2009 burdened with about as much hype as any teenager could have. After all, how many guys break a Fisher-Price rim when they're 3, dunk for real over an opponent at 14, or are a sure bet to move from high school directly to the NBA — had it been allowed? But since it wasn't, Wall spent his one season of college ball in Lexington.

The Kentucky coaches quickly learned some things about their prized freshman. Like that goal, for instance, and his willingness to work to achieve it. "I did not know his work ethic," said head Cat John Calipari. "And I've been surprised."

Calipari also learned of Wall's overarching desire not just to be great individually but to win as a team. "I did not know his will to win was this strong," he said. As assistant coach Rod Strickland put it, "As soon as the ball goes up, [Wall's] a different person. He's a killer out there."

The Wall legend began in his first game when he hit a buzzer-beater to whip Miami (Ohio). He scored 25 points in a 64-61 win over UConn on Dec. 9. On Dec. 29, he set the Wildcat single-game assist record with 16, breaking Travis Ford's standard of 15.

When the 2009-10 season ended, Wall had set a new Kentucky record for assists in a season (241) and points by a freshman. He was the SEC Player of the Year, the tournament MVP, and a First-Team All-America. Yahoo! Sports named him its National Player of the Year. In April 2010, he became the first Wildcat player to be drafted first overall by the NBA. He had achieved his goal of being the nation's best collegiate point guard.

And about that goal Wall had of winning? The Cats of 2009-10 went a sensational 35-3, won the SEC Tournament, and made it to the Elite Eight in the NCAA tournament.

What are your goals? Have you ever thought them out? Or do you just shuffle along living for your paycheck and whatever fun you can seek out instead of pursuing some greater purpose?

Now try this one: What is the goal of your faith life? You go to church to worship God. You read the Bible and study God's word to learn about God and how God wants you to live. But what is it you hope to achieve? What is all that stuff about? For what purpose do you believe that Jesus Christ is God's son?

The answer is actually quite simple: The goal of your faith life is your salvation, and this is the only goal in life that matters. Nothing you will ever seek is as important or as eternal as getting into Heaven and making sure that everybody you know and love will be there too one day.

If I ever accomplish [a goal], I'll set a higher goal and go after that.
— *Bobby Bowden*

**The most important goal of your life is
to get to Heaven and to help as many people
as you can to get there one day too.**

IN THE KNOW

Read John 4:19-26, 39-42.

"They said to the woman, . . . 'Now we have heard for ourselves, and we know that this man really is the Savior of the world'" (v. 42).

Kentucky's Albert Kirwan just had to know something — and the answer he got was a strange one.

Kirwan was "a big Irishman with the features of a scholarly prize fighter, the morals of an apostle, and the nerve to accept the position of football coach" at UK. He took the job in 1938, some time after starring at UK in track and as a halfback and an end. As a senior in 1925, he captained the football team. He was a history professor at the university, eventually serving as Dean of Students and Dean of the Graduate School.

Throughout his life, among Kirwan's most vivid memories was the Centre game of 1923 when he suffered through his most miserable performance on the gridiron. As a sophomore, he was the team's left halfback on Nov. 3 when the 4-0-1 Wildcats met the Colonels. The school's new stadium was dedicated that day before "a crowd of 10,000 of the wettest fans who ever witnessed a football game."

That Centre team was the undisputed champions of the South, beating the likes of Alabama and Georgia. On this day, they defeated the Cats, too, 10-0. Kirwan did little offensively to help his team out; he was nailed so often in the backfield that his rushing average for the day was -2 yards per carry.

Kirwan never could figure out how Centre was able to stop him so completely even though the muddy field had slowed him down. Years later he found out why — or at least he got an explanation that he had to accept no matter how implausible it was.

One day he ran into the Centre fullback. Still worried about his dismal showing, Kirwan asked him what had happened. The player replied, "After the first few plays when the color of our uniforms was completely obliterated by the mud, our two guards would line up with your team and simply turn around and tackle you."

Now Kirwan knew.

You know certain things in your life too. That your spouse loves you, for instance. That you are good at your job. That tea should be iced and sweetened. That a bad day fishing is still better than a good day at work. You know these things even though no mathematician or philosopher can prove any of this on paper.

It's the same way with faith in Jesus: You just know that he is God's son and the savior of the world. You know it in the same way that you know UK is the only team worth pulling for: with every fiber of your being, with all your heart, your mind, and your soul. You know it despite the mindless babble and blasphemy of the unbelievers.

You just know, and because you know him, Jesus knows you. And that is all you really need to know.

I'm inclined to believe he might have been telling the truth.
— Ab Kirwan on the answer about the Centre game

A life of faith is lived in certainty and conviction:
You just know you know.

NAME DROPPING

Read Exodus 3:13-20.

"God said to Moses, 'I AM WHO I AM. This is what you are to say to the Israelites: 'I AM has sent me to you'" *(v. 14).*

Swoop. Bug Eye. Master Blaster aka The Phantom. When guys with nicknames like that contribute, how can the Cats lose?

The Cats of 1987-88 took part in the first-ever Big Four Classic. On Dec. 5, before 43,601 fans in the Hoosier Dome and a national TV audience, Kentucky played Indiana in an instant classic.

Among the UK heroes was 6-9 senior forward Cedric Cortrell Jenkins, who bore the downright delightful nickname "Swoop." "As far as I can tell, it's because of my arms," Jenkins explained. It made sense; his wing span was "a pterodactyl-like 79 inches."

Jenkins "had averaged a no-factor 2.1 points" in his career. On this day, though, he was virtually perfect. He finished five of five from the field and four of four from the line and grabbed ten rebounds to go with a couple of blocks and assists.

Wildcat forward Winston Bennett's fifth foul with 6:11 to play and the game tied at 59 sent Richard "Master Blaster" Madison onto the floor. The nickname was actually a misnomer as "Master hadn't blasted a soul" in three seasons. Head coach Eddie Sutton had labeled him "a phantom."

And then there was guard Ed "Bug Eye" Davender, who wore his moniker before he played in goggles to protect a detached

WILDCATS

retina. With Kentucky leading 78-76 in overtime, "Bug Eye," who poured in 22 points, forced a Hoosier into losing his dribble. Rex Chapman dived for the ball and, as he was falling, passed it to none other than . . . the phantom himself. Master Blaster let loose with a thunderous dunk with 34 seconds left to play. When Indiana missed, he came down with the rebound.

Thanks in part to Swoop, Bug Eye, and Master Blaster, the Cats had a thrilling 82-76 overtime win over the mighty Hoosiers.

Nicknames such as "Swoop" and "Bug Eye" often reflect rather widely held perceptions about the person named. Proper names do that also. Nowhere throughout history has this concept been more prevalent than in the Bible, where a name is not a mere label but is an expression of the essential nature of the named one. That is, a person's name reveals his or her character.

Even God shares this concept; to know the name of God is to know God as he has chosen to reveal himself to us.

What does your name say about you? Honest, trustworthy, a seeker of the truth and a person of God? Or does the mention of your name cause your coworkers to whisper snide remarks, your neighbors to roll their eyes, or your friends to start making allowances for you? Most importantly, what does your name say about you to God? He, too, knows you by name.

A good nickname inspires awe and ensures that you'll be enshrined in the Pantheon of [Sports] Legends.
> — *Funny Sports Quotes blog*

**Live so that your name evokes positive
associations by people you know,
by the public, and by God.**

THE GREATEST

Read Mark 9:33-37.

"If anyone wants to be first, he must be the very last, and the servant of all" (v. 35).

They are the greatest, at least according to *Sports Illustrated*, which in 2007 picked an all-time UK women's basketball team.

SI staff writer William F. Read cited the coinciding of the hiring of coach Matthew Mitchell, a former UK assistant under Mickie De-Moss, and the new state-of-the-art practice facility as a good time to name the program's greatest. In the wake of the careers of All-American Victoria Dunlap, guard Samantha Mahoney, and guard A'dia Matthies, however, the list may well need some updating.

Dunlap was the 2011 SEC Player of the Year and the league's Defensive Player of the Year. Mahoney ended her playing days in 2008 as the program's No. 4 all- time leading scorer. Matthies was twice the SEC Player of the Year (2011 and 2012), set the UK record for career steals, and finished second in career points.

With the Dunlap-Mahoney-Matthies caveat in place, here is *SI*'s all-time greatest UK women's team.

The team starts with center Valerie Still (1979-83). Her 2,763 points is still the record for career points scored by a UK player, man or woman. In '83, she led Kentucky to its highest national ranking — #4 — in history. She was the only female athlete inducted into the charter class of the UK Athletics Hall of Fame.

According to *SI*, the greatest Wildcat forwards are Leslie

Nichols (1982-86) and Bebe Croley (1984-88). Nichols still stands fourth all-time in both career points and career rebounds. She was inducted into the UK Hall of Fame in 2013. Croley averaged 14.2 points and 6.4 rebounds per game in her career.

The all-time UK guards are Patty Jo Hedges (1979-83) and Sara Potts (2001-05). Hedges holds the career school record with 731 assists. Potts holds the UK career record for treys made (271).

All together, they are the greatest.

We all want to be the greatest in whatever we do. The goal for the Cats and their fans every season is the national championship. The competition at work is to be the most productive salesperson on the staff or the Teacher of the Year. In other words, we define being the greatest in terms of the struggle for personal success. It's nothing new; Jesus' disciples saw greatness in the same way.

As Jesus illustrated, though, greatness in the Kingdom of God has nothing to do with the secular world's understanding of success. Rather, the greatest are those who channel their ambition toward the furtherance of Christ's kingdom through love and service, rather than their own advancement, which is a complete reversal of status and values as the world sees them.

After all, who could be greater than the person who has Jesus for a brother and God for a father? And that's every one of us.

There's no reason why we can't be one of the premier programs in the nation.
— UK women's basketball head coach Matthew Mitchell

To be great for God has nothing to do
with personal advancement and everything to do
with the advancement of Christ's kingdom.

DAY 8

FEAR FACTOR

Read Matthew 14:22-33.

"[The disciples] cried out in fear. But Jesus immediately said to them: 'Take courage! It is I. Don't be afraid'" (vv. 26-27).

Man, my team's playing scared." Kentucky sure wasn't even though the Cats were playing the nation's top-ranked team.

On Feb. 4, 2003, the Florida Gators, ranked No. 1 in the country and riding a 14-game win streak, slithered into Rupp Arena to take on the sixth-ranked Wildcats, who were 16-3 and had reeled off ten straight wins of their own. The largest crowd in Rupp Arena history awaited them. So did a Kentucky team so ferocious and so intense that the Gator point guard admitted to UK senior guard Keith Bogans during the game that his team was afraid.

The only fear on the Wildcats' side was that displayed by head coach Tubby Smith. He just couldn't look at the scoreboard, not even in the second half, as though his eyeballing the score might change it. He would ask one of the players or his coaches what the margin was, but "That's it," Smith said.

He knew what was going on, though, even if it surprised him, the players, and the fans and frightened the Gators into meek submission. "As much as it surprised the spectators, it surprised us, too," admitted forward Chuck Hayes. "We were expecting war."

They didn't get it. Instead, the Cats rolled to a 23-point lead at halftime and led by as many as 29 in the second half before winning by the deceptive final score of 70-55.

Even Florida's head coach admitted his seniors got rattled when the Wildcats went on a 21-2 run late in the first half. In the last thirteen minutes of the half, Florida missed 17 of 18 shots.

The Kentucky players saw what was happening. "I know they said coming to Rupp wasn't a big deal, but you could see it was," observed UK center Jules Camara.

"We were just out there having fun," Hayes declared. "Tonight was all about having fun." For the Gators, it was all about fear.

Some fears are universal; others are particular. Speaking to a local civic club may call for an extra heavy dose of antiperspirant. Elevator walls may feel as though they're closing in on you. And don't even get started on being in the dark with spiders and snakes during a thunderstorm.

We all live in fear, and God knows this. Dozens of passages in the Bible urge us not to be afraid. God isn't telling us to lose our wariness of oncoming cars or big dogs with nasty dispositions; this is a helpful fear God instilled in us for protection.

What God does wish driven from our lives is a spirit of fear that dominates us, that makes our lives miserable and keeps us from doing what we should, such as sharing our faith. In commanding that we not be afraid, God reminds us that when we trust completely in him, we find peace that calms our fears.

Let me win. But if I cannot win, let me be brave in the attempt.
— Special Olympics Motto

You have your own peculiar set of fears,
but they should never paralyze you
because God is greater than anything you fear.

DAY 9

HERO WORSHIP

Read 1 Samuel 16:1-13.

"Do not consider his appearance or his height, for . . . the Lord does not look at the things man looks at. . . . The Lord looks at the heart" (v. 7).

John Simms "Shipwreck" Kelly was not just a hero on the gridiron but was a hero in real life also.

Kelly was "a talented athlete with a charismatic personality" who was All-America in track and football at UK in 1931 and '32. He was described as "a big, handsome swaggering star" and "a flamboyant person with a flair for the spectacular." He used that flamboyance to cut a path through college athletics that turned him into one of the era's biggest sports heroes.

For instance, on the eve of the 1931 Alabama game, Kelly met reporters in his hotel room sitting on his bed wearing a pair of shorts. He said, "Gentlemen, tomorrow, I will make a touchdown against Alabama. It will be more than 50 yards long." It was 57.

The same season Tennessee and Tulane were vying for a spot in the Rose Bowl. Kelly sent a telegram to the Tulane head coach that read, "Make your plans to go to the Rose Bowl for we will take care of Tennessee for you tomorrow." Kelly rushed for 117 yards in a 6-6 tie. Tulane went to the Rose Bowl.

When UK crushed Virginia 47-0 in 1930, both coaches started their second teams. Late in the game, the crowd started screaming for Kelly, who entered the game and went 65 yards for a TD on his first play.

Kelly was a hero in real life, too. In 1959, he was credited with herding dozens of people to safety during a hotel fire in Rome. Wearing a green bathrobe and slippers, he repeatedly "rushed up the stairs to the smoke-filled upper floors to find guests."

Despite his gridiron heroics and the lives he helped save in the fire, Kelly for years was concerned that people would see him as a "draft-dodging football hero" because a broken leg that did not heal properly kept him out of World War II. Instead, he worked undercover for the FBI during the war.

A hero is thought of as someone who performs brave and dangerous feats that save or protect someone's life — as John Simms "Shipwreck" Kelly did. You figure that excludes you.

But ask your son about that when you show him how to bait a hook, or your daughter when you show her how to hit a softball. Look into the eyes of those Little Leaguers you help coach.

Ask God about heroism when you're steady in your faith. For God, a hero is a person with the heart of a servant. And if a hero is a servant who acts to save other's lives, then the greatest hero of all is Jesus Christ.

God seeks heroes today, those who will proclaim the name of their hero — Jesus — proudly and boldly, no matter how others may scoff or ridicule. God knows heroes when he sees them — by what's in their hearts.

Heroes and cowards feel exactly the same fear; heroes just act differently.
— Boxing trainer Cus D'Amato

God's heroes are those who remain steady
in their faith while serving others.

DAY 10

COMEBACK KIDS

Read Luke 23:26-43.

"Jesus answered him, 'I tell you the truth, today you will be with me in paradise'" (v. 43).

The comeback was so stunning that it matched the greatest one in NCAA Division I history.

On Feb. 15, 1994, in Baton Rouge, the 11th-ranked Wildcats were big favorites over an LSU team that was described as "SEC West also-rans." Well, they ran all right, nearly running the Cats out of the gym and leading by 16 points at halftime. Still, UK head man Rick Pitino remained confident at the break. "He just made some adjustments and reminded us never to give up," said guard Chris Harrison.

That confidence took a severe beating when the Tigers scored 18 straight points early in the second half to lead by 31 at 68-37 with fifteen minutes left. Pitino called a time out "and just glared at us," Harrison said. Then he told Harrison to go into the game. Senior point guard Travis Ford told him, "You're gonna light it up tonight."

Harrison did. He hit a pair of treys, "and all of a sudden everybody seemed to get in on the act," he recalled. "We started raining threes just the way they had in the first half."

Harrison scored eight quick points in a 24-4 UK run that cut the margin to 11 points with 10 minutes to play. That avalanche of three-pointers — twelve the last half — and tough defense let the Cats keep chipping away at the seemingly insurmountable LSU lead.

LSU led only 95-90 with 1:40 to play when Tony Delk hit a trey. Forward Walter McCarty, who hadn't hit a three-pointer in the last eight games, swished one with 19 seconds to play. The Cats led 96-95.

Kentucky scored the last nine points of the game and won 99-95. The comeback tied the Division I record for most points overcome in the second half to win.

Life will have its setbacks whether they result from personal failures or from forces and people beyond your control. Being a Christian and a faithful follower of Jesus Christ doesn't insulate you from getting into deep trouble. Maybe financial problems suffocated you. A debilitating illness struck you. Or a great tragedy hit your family. Life is a series of victories and defeats. Winning isn't about avoiding defeat; it's about getting back up to compete again. It's about making a comeback of your own.

When you avail yourself of God's grace and God's power, your comeback is always greater than your setback. You are never too far behind, and it's never too late in life's game for Jesus to lead you to victory, to turn trouble into triumph.

As it was with the Wildcats against LSU in '94 and with the thief on the cross who repented, it's not how you start that counts; it's how you finish.

You guys are gonna pay for this tomorrow in practice.
— *Rick Pitino to the Cats when they trailed LSU by 31*

In life, victory is truly a matter of how you finish and whether you finish with Jesus at your side.

MEMORY LOSS

Read 1 Corinthians 11:17-29.

"[D]o this in remembrance of me" (v. 24).

The Wildcats remembered, and the Volunteers paid for it.

On Feb. 7, 2006, Tennessee toppled Kentucky at Rupp Arena. What followed was an unseemly celebration by the Volunteer head coach that included his ripping off his shirt. The Kentucky players and coaches stored that insulting revelry in their memory banks and pulled it out for inspiration when they traveled to Knoxville less than a month later.

After falling behind the 11th-ranked Vols by 14 points in the first half, the Wildcats rallied by scorching the nets in the last half with 15 of 19 shooting. Their four misses came on three-pointers. Kentucky never trailed over the last 15:20 of the game, but Tennessee hung tough by nailing a series of treys. Sophomore guard Joe Crawford's three with 4:26 left broke a 73-73 tie and propelled the Cats into the lead for good.

In the closing seconds, though, the Cats committed a pair of turnovers that gave Tennessee a chance with UK leading 80-78. A big steal by senior guard Brandon Stockton ultimately forced the Vols to throw up a last-gasp shot that bounced off the rim as the horn sounded.

That touched off a raucous Wildcat celebration rendered especially sweet in light of what had happened in Lexington. Let the record show, though, that head coach Tubby Smith did not rip off

WILDCATS

his shirt though he did share high-fives with the Cat fans who lined the exit to the locker room. And the Cats celebrated noisily in the privacy of their locker room, not on the court.

The players engulfed senior guard Patrick Sparks in a group cheer, and he became so excited that he bounced a chair against the locker-room wall. "It was crazy in there," commented forward Rekalin Sims.

All it all, it was a night for the Wildcats to remember.

Memory makes us who we are. Whether our memories appear as pleasant reverie or unnerving nightmares, they shape us and to a large extent determine both our actions and our reactions. Alzheimer's is so terrifying because it steals our memory from us, and in the process we lose ourselves. We disappear.

The greatest tragedy of our lives is that God remembers. In response to that photographic memory, he condemns us for our sins. Paradoxically, the greatest joy of our lives is that God remembers. In response to that memory, he came as Jesus to wash even the memory of our sins away.

Through memory, we encounter revival. At the Last Supper, Jesus instructed his disciples and us to remember. In sharing this unique meal with fellow believers and remembering Jesus and his actions, we meet Christ again, not just as a memory but as an actual living presence. To remember is to keep our faith alive.

I don't want them to forget Babe Ruth. I just want them to remember Hank Aaron.

— Hank Aaron

**We remember Jesus,
and God will not remember our sins.**

DAY 12

SEEING THE VISION

Read Acts 26:1, 9-23.

"So then, . . . I was not disobedient to the vision from heaven" (v. 19).

Joe B. Hall must have had a miraculous vision that day." It certainly seemed that way, but the Kentucky head coach had just craftily set events up so they transpired just as he said they would.

Hall was the head coach of the Wildcats for thirteen seasons from 1972-85. His 1978 squad won the school's fifth national title. His overall record at Kentucky was 297-100.

His 1974-75 team met Indiana in the Midwest Regional finals of the NCAA Tournament. The Hoosiers were undefeated and were ranked No. 1. Moreover, they had brutalized the Cats 98-74 back on Dec. 7.

This night was to be different, though, as UK won a thriller 92-90. Hall revealed his four-part, apparently miraculous vision to his players in the locker room prior to the game. First, he told them to be careful with the scissors when they were cutting down the nets. Second, he described to them how the team bus would be met by the highway patrol when it crossed the state line.

Third, he said, they would have a police escort all the way to Lexington. He described how Interstate 75 would be lined with cars where folks had pulled over to cheer for their heroes. He said the overpasses would be decorated with signs and banners.

Finally, he predicted Lexington police would pick them up at the city limits and lead them to Memorial Coliseum where thousands of ecstatic fans would welcome them home.

To the players' shock, everything turned out just exactly the way their visionary coach had predicted. Only sometime later did Hall reveal the truth. On his post-game radio show, he had related to announcer Cawood Ledford everything he had predicted to his players. The highway patrol heard it, the fans headed home on I-75 heard it, the Lexington police heard it, and students and fans everywhere heard it. They all acted accordingly.

To speak of visions is often to risk their being lumped with palm readings, Ouija boards, seances, horoscopes, and other such useless mumbo-jumbo. The danger such mild amusements pose, however, is very real in that they indicate a reliance on something other than God. It is God who knows the future; it is God who has a vision and a plan for your life; it is God who has the answers you seek as you struggle to find your way.

You probably do have a vision for your life, a plan for how it should unfold. It's the dream you pursue through your family, your job, your hobbies, your interests. But your vision inspires a fruitful life only if it is compatible with God's plan. As the apostle Paul found out, you ignore God's vision at your peril. But if you pursue it, you'll find an even more glorious life than you could ever have envisioned for yourself.

NETS, BUS, POLICE, COLISEUM.
— The words Joe B. Hall wrote on the board prior to the Indiana game

**Your grandest vision for the future pales
beside the vision God has of what the two of you
can accomplish together.**

DAY 13

IN THE BAD TIMES

Read Philippians 1:3-14.

"What has happened to me has really served to advance the gospel. . . . Because of my chains, most of the brothers in the Lord have been encouraged to speak the word of God more courageously and fearlessly" (vv. 12, 14).

The year 1897 was a bad time for the Kentucky State College football program: The team "was without question the worst State had produced up to that time" and the stadium burned down.

Football in Lexington in '97 was still "harem-scarem," according to D.D. Slade, an end on that squad. Teams still sometimes played their own coaches and often borrowed players from the opponent to complete the lineup. Slade didn't recall many practices, saying, "We just got in and played the best way we could." The team still played without helmets or padding.

As one writer put it, "If ever a team needed help, it was that 1897 crew." They didn't start off so badly, sitting at 2-1 after three games. But then came three solid defeats: Vanderbilt 50-0, Central 18-0, and Centre College 36-0. Play was so bad that "rumors persisted that [the team] would be disbanded."

Matters got worse when the covered grandstand at the football field burned down. Someone had carelessly stored some lime under the stands, a rainstorm came up, and the barrels caught fire. By daylight, the grandstands were history. Only a short while later, the fence around the field started falling to pieces.

WILDCATS

These were both "modest structures, [but] there were no funds to replace them." The students had no solution to the money problem, so the future of football at the school was indeed in doubt until the faculty stepped in and assumed greater control of athletics through a faculty committee.

In 1898, the football team was not only undefeated and untied, but was unscored on. For a while at least, the bad times were over.

Loved ones die. You're downsized. Your biopsy looks cancerous. Your house burns down. Hard, tragic times are as much a part of life as breath.

This applies to Christians too. Christianity is not the equivalent of a Get-out-of-Jail-Free card, granting us a lifelong exemption from either the least or the worst pain the world has to offer. While Jesus promises us he will be there to lead us through the valleys, he never promises that we will not enter them.

The question therefore becomes how you handle the bad times. You can buckle to your knees in despair and cry, "Why me?" Or you can hit your knees in prayer and ask, "What do I do with this?"

Setbacks and tragedies are opportunities to reveal and to develop both true character and abiding faith. Your faithfulness — not your skipping merrily along through life without pain — is what reveals the depth of your love for God.

The game I remember most was the Vanderbilt game. They beat the tar out of us. They ran all over the top of us.
— *D.D. Slade on the 1897 Vandy game*

**Faithfulness to God requires faith
even in — especially in — the bad times.**

TRAGEDY

Read Job 1, 2:1-10.

"In all this, Job did not sin by charging God with wrongdoing" (v. 1:22).

Tragedy changed DeAndre Liggins' life.

Growing up on the mean streets of the South Side of Chicago, Liggins never imagined himself as a college basketball player. "I played ball, but I only played on the playground," he said. That dream was for his older brother, Maurice Davis. In 2003, he was a high-school senior and a basketball star being recruited by the likes of Kansas. Liggins figured he'd watch his brother playing college ball; that road was not one he'd walk down.

Then Davis was shot and killed in a dispute with their sister's ex-boyfriend. Liggins' father died that same year. Sobered by the deaths, Liggins looked around at his neighborhood, in particular at some of his cousins. "They're just in the streets, hanging out, not doing anything with their lives," he said. He promised himself he would not follow that path.

In his grief, he turned to his grandmother and to basketball. She moved him out of the projects, and the game became Liggins' passion. "I tried to follow [Maurice's] dream and stick with basketball because I know he did," Liggins said. I wanted to continue [my brother's] dream." He became a high-school star as Maurice had been, and Kentucky came calling.

His game is always a tribute to his brother. He has a tattoo of

Davis' face on his right shoulder, and at UK, he wore jersey number 34, which was his brother's number in high school. Then as a junior in 2010-11, he paid his brother the ultimate tribute: He became a driving force for a UK team that made an unexpected run to the Final Four. He was then drafted by the Orlando Magic.

DeAndre Liggins turned a tragedy into personal triumph.

While we may receive them in varying degrees, suffering and tragedy are par for life's course. What we do with tragedy when it strikes us — as DeAndre Liggins' story illustrates — determines to a great extent how we live the rest of our lives.

We can — in accordance with the bitter suggestion Job's wife offered — "Curse God and die," or we can trust God and live. That is, we can plunge into endless despair or we can lean upon the power of a transcendent faith in an almighty God who offers us hope in our darkest hours.

We don't have to understand tragedy; we certainly don't have to like it or believe there's anything fair about it. What we must do in such times, however, is trust in God's all-powerful love for us and his promise that all things will work for good for those who love him.

In choosing a life of ongoing trust in God in the face of our suffering, we prevent the greatest tragedy of all: that of a soul being cast into Hell.

I know my brother looks down on me. When adversity swarmed my way, I held my head high. I'm just happy about that.
— DeAndre Liggins on the tragedy that changed his life

Tragedy can drive us into despair and death or into the life-sustaining arms of almighty God.

NEVER TOO LATE

Read John 11:17-27, 38-44.

"'But, Lord," said Martha, . . . "he has been there four days.' Then Jesus said, 'Did I not tell you that if you believed, you would see the glory of God?'" (vv. 19b-40)

Twenty-five years after he last played for Kentucky, Mike Casey finally got his championship ring.

Casey was First-Team All-SEC as a sophomore and as a junior (1967-69). "In all the years of Kentucky basketball, . . . it's possible the Wildcats have never been more promising than the summer before [the] 1969-70 season." Casey, UK legend Dan Issel, and All-American Mike Pratt were all returning as seniors.

But then that summer Casey almost died.

Driving into Lexington for a pickup basketball game, his car rammed into a utility pole. It broke off and speared him in the left leg. He was fortunate the pole had not been higher, but the damage was bad enough. Only when a reporter called Casey's hospital room did he learn the injury was career-threatening. In New York when he learned of the accident, Coach Adolph Rupp declared, "There goes the national championship."

He was right. Casey redshirted the 1969-70 season. The Cats were ranked No. 1 heading into the NCAA Tournament but lost in the second round. With Casey in the game — well, the outcome may well have been quite different.

Casey returned in 1970-71, but both the team and he were dif-

WILDCATS

ferent. Issel and Pratt had graduated, and Casey's left leg had now deprived him of his explosive first step. Again, the Cats fell in the second round of the NCAA Tournament.

Mike Casey's horrific accident may well have cost what would have been one of UK's greatest teams the 1970 title. But Casey did get a ring. After UK won the 1996 title, Casey sold them their title rings. Coach Rick Pitino ordered an extra one — for Casey.

Getting that college degree. Getting married. Starting a new career. Though we may make all kinds of excuses, it's often never too late for life-changing decisions and milestones.

This is especially true in our faith life, which is based on God's promises through Jesus Christ. Jesus showed up in Bethany four days late, as Martha pointed out, having seemingly dawdled a little as though the death of his friend Lazarus really didn't matter to him. It clearly did since he broke down and cried when he saw Lazarus' burial site. Being Jesus, however, he wasn't late; he was right on time because with Jesus there are no impossible situations or circumstances.

This is true in our own lives no matter how hopeless our current circumstances may appear to us. At any time — today even — we can regret the things we have done wrong and the way we have lived, ask God in Jesus' name to forgive us for them, and discover a new way of living — forever.

With Jesus, it's never too late.

It's never too late to achieve success in sports.
— Brooke de Lench, writer and lecturer on children and sports

It's never too late to change a life
by turning it over to Jesus.

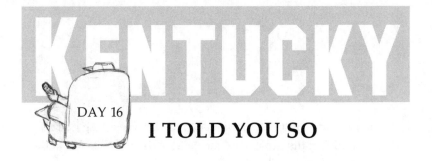

I TOLD YOU SO

Read Matthew 24:15-31.

"See, I have told you ahead of time" (v. 25).

Son, you're not good enough to play for us." So said the coach to the recruit. "I told you so." So said the recruit to the coach.

UK head baseball coach John Cohen (2004-08) was once quite frank with a high-school junior. "I tried to talk him out of coming to Kentucky," he recalled. He was actually more blunt than that. As Collin Cowgill remembered it, Cohen told him, "I don't know if you're going to be able to play here." In other words, you're not good enough to play in Lexington.

Cohen liked Cowgill, but this was 2004, and the new coach on campus had inherited a program short on talent. So he saw in Cowgill a nice kid who was well liked in the community and who was "coming off a junior year that was solid, but not by SEC standards in recruiting." Cohen needed some SEC-caliber ball players, so he told Cowgill he'd be better off pursuing other options.

Cowgill didn't appreciate it. "Coach Cohen lit a fire under me," he said. He hit the weight room, had a magnificent senior season, and committed to Kentucky — on an academic scholarship.

True to Cohen's expectations, Cowgill didn't do too much his freshman season, but he broke out his sophomore year, hitting .298 with 16 homers and 61 RBIs. He was a key part of Kentucky's first-ever SEC champions. A hand injury sidelined him in 2007, but even so the Oakland A's drafted him. He decided to return to

Kentucky for his senior season in 2008, and the result was an All-American year as he hit .361 with 19 homers and 60 RBIs.

During the season, Cohen fessed up, saying of the player whom he had disparaged, "He's one of the best outfielders in college baseball." For Cowgill's part, he never missed a chance to poke fun at what he called his coach's "lack of recruitment." That is, he took every opportunity he could to say to Cohen, "I told you so."

In July 2011, Cowgill, the player who wasn't good enough, made his major league debut with the Arizona Diamondbacks.

Don't you just hate it in when somebody says, "I told you so"? That means the other person was right and you were wrong; that other person has spoken the truth. You could have listened to that know-it-all in the first place, but then you would have lost the chance yourself to crow, "I told you so."

In our pluralistic age and society, many view truth as relative, meaning absolute truth does not exist. All belief systems have equal value and merit. But this is a ghastly, dangerous fallacy because it ignores the truth that God proclaimed in the presence and words of Jesus.

In speaking the truth, Jesus told everybody exactly what he was going to do: come back and take his faithful followers with him. Those who don't listen or who don't believe will be left behind with those four awful words, "I told you so," ringing in their ears and wringing their souls.

I dedicated myself to proving [Coach John Cohen] wrong.
— Collin Cowgill

Jesus matter-of-factly told us what he has planned:
He will return to gather all the faithful to himself.

DAY 17

SMILING FACES

Read Philippians 4:4-7.

"Rejoice in the Lord always. I will say it again: Rejoice!"
(v. 4)

John Calipari turned, hugged an assistant, and let fly with one big old grin. And why not? He had just won his first-ever national title as a head coach.

The Kentucky Wildcats of 2011-12 illustrated just how much the landscape of college basketball has changed. Calipari assembled a team of superstars, starting with the nation's top recruiting class of forwards Michael Kidd-Gilchrist and Anthony Davis and guard Marquis Teague. Three key players returned from the Final Four team of 2011: Terrence Jones, Doran Lamb, and Darius Miller.

The team took the floor for the first time on Nov. 15 carrying heavy expectations. With only one shot before players bolted for the NBA, the season would be considered less than successful with anything short of a Final Four berth.

Behind the motto "Blue Together," Calipari worked to mold this band of exceptional players into an exceptional team. On April 2, it all came together in New Orleans with the finals of the NCAA Tournament.

"We want to win a title," Davis said of this mix of players from Oregon to New Jersey and compass points in between. And they did just that.

They whipped Kansas 67-59 for Kentucky's eighth national

WILDCATS

title and Calipari's first. They did it playing Kansas' game. The Jayhawks wanted to outmuscle the Cats, so play on the floor was tough and gritty.

It didn't make any difference. Kentucky took the lead on a Teague jumper with 16:42 left in the first half. The Cats never trailed again, leading 41-27 at the break.

They wobbled for a moment as Kansas rallied to within 62-57 with only 1:37 left, but Kidd-Gilchrist blocked a shot to shut down the Jayhawks' last threat.

The celebration of a national championship began. And so did John Calipari's smiles.

What does your smile say about you? What is it that makes you smile and laugh in the first place? Your dad's corny jokes? Don Knotts as Barney Fife? Your children or grandchildren? Your pal's bad imitations? Do you hoard your smile or do you give it away easily even when you've had some tough times?

When you smile, the ones who love you and whom you love can't help but return the favor — and the joy. It's like turning on a bright light in a world threatened by darkness.

Besides, you have good reason to walk around all the time with a smile on your face not because of something you have done but rather because of one basic, unswerving truth: God loves you. Because of his love for you, God acted through Jesus to give you free and eternal salvation. That should certainly make you smile.

We were the best team.
 — *A smiling John Calipari after the title-clinching win over Kansas*

**It's so overused it's become a cliché,
but it's true nevertheless: Smile! God loves you.**

MAKE NO MISTAKE

Read Mark 14:66-72.

"Then Peter remembered the word Jesus had spoken to him: 'Before the rooster crows twice you will disown me three times.' And he broke down and wept" (v. 72).

Key mistakes cost the Wildcats a pair of losses; mistakes then helped them win a big one.

Kentucky head football coach Guy Morriss had it figured out in 2002: His team had to stop shooting itself in the foot to win games. The Cats were 4-2 after back-to-back losses in which UK helped the opposition with a series of "key mistakes and mental breakdowns."

"For the last two weeks we have been preaching to them that we have to eliminate mistakes," Morriss said after the second loss. So the Cats went out and played mistake-free ball against Arkansas on Oct. 19 and took home a win, right? Not at all. In fact, a series of first-half blunders led to a 10-9 Arkansas lead at halftime.

Then the tables turned the last half. UK safety Mike Williams intercepted a Hog pass on the first play of the half and returned it to the Arkansas 12. On the next play, running back Artose Pinner scored to put UK on top 16-10.

Arkansas then made a special-teams mistake. After the defense held, Derek Abney returned a Hog punt 86 yards to make it 22-10. In less than four minutes, the Cats had run only one offensive play and had turned a one-point deficit into a 12-point lead.

The mistakes kept coming. After Arkansas made it a 22-17 game, Tommy Cook fell on a Hog fumble at their 17. Jared Lorenzen and Aaron Boone followed up by turning a screen pass into a touchdown that put the final score of 29-17 on the board.

"We had too many mistakes," lamented the Hog head coach. And for once, mistakes helped the Cats to a big road win.

It's distressing but it's true: Like football teams and Simon Peter, we all make mistakes. Only one perfect man ever walked on this earth, and no one of us is he. Some mistakes are just dumb. Like locking yourself out of your car or falling into a swimming pool with your clothes on.

Other mistakes are more significant. Like heading down a path to addiction. Committing a crime. Walking out on a spouse and the children.

All these mistakes, however, from the momentarily annoying to the life-altering tragic, share one aspect: They can all be forgiven in Christ. Other folks may not forgive us; we may not even forgive ourselves. But God will forgive us when we call upon him in Jesus' name.

Thus, the twofold fatal mistake we can make is ignoring the fact that we will die one day and subsequently ignoring the fact that Jesus is the only way to shun Hell and enter Heaven. We absolutely must get this one right.

We had made every mistake you could possibly make in a football game and were only down by one point.
— Guy Morriss on the 2002 Arkansas game

Only one mistake we make sends us to Hell
when we die: ignoring Jesus while we live.

IMPRESSIONS

Read Mark 6:1-6.

"And [Jesus] was amazed at their lack of faith" (v. 6).

Sean Woods made quite a first impression on his team's new strength and conditioning coach: He threw up.

Woods was a starring member of the Unforgettables, the 1992 team that won the SEC and lost to Duke in the East Regional final that many consider the greatest game in college basketball history. He scored 21 points in the game, and his improbable running 10-footer with 2.9 seconds left gave the Cats a 103-102 lead.

During the summer of 1989 after Rick Pitino took over the program, Woods dropped by the new head man's office. Pitino introduced him to Rock Oliver, the team's new strength and conditioning coach. Woods said, "It was obvious that this Oliver guy was salivating over the opportunity to get started putting the players through their paces, and I was the only player around."

So the pair headed down to the court. There, Oliver introduced the player to what Woods said was "a machine kind of like a lawn mower except that pushing that thing was like pushing a car in neutral." The coach challenged Woods: "Let's see if you can push it the length of the court down and back 18 times."

Wanting to make a good first impression, Woods went to work. "I was dying after about five times," he said, but he wasn't about to let Oliver know it; he just kept pushing.

He made it — 18 times — but when he sat down with Oliver, he started feeling sick. He spotted a garbage can, and, still wanting to impress the coach, nonchalantly made his way to it. "I couldn't let Rock know how desperate I was," he said. "I just barely made it to that garbage can."

Perhaps he hadn't made such a great first impression on his coach, but Oliver had certainly made one on him.

You bought that canary convertible mainly to impress the girls; a white Accord would transport you more efficiently. You seek out subtle but effective ways to gain the boss' approval. You may be all grown up now, but you still want your parents' favor. You dress professionally but strikingly and always take your prospective clients to that overpriced steak house.

In our lives we are constantly seeking to impress someone else so they'll remember us and respond favorably to us. That's exactly the impression we should be making upon Jesus because in God's scheme for salvation, only the good opinion of Jesus Christ matters. On the day when we stand before God, our fate for eternity rests upon Jesus remembering and responding favorably to us.

We don't want to be like the folks in Jesus' hometown. Oh, they impressed him all right: with their lack of faith in him. This is not the impression we want to make.

I left the gym that day knowing my teammates and I were in for the most grueling preseason camp of our lives.
— Sean Woods on his first impression of Rock Oliver

Jesus is the only one worth impressing,
and it is the depth of your faith
— or the lack of it — that impresses him.

DAY 20

DREAM WORLD

Read Joshua 3.

"All Israel passed by until the whole nation had completed the crossing on dry ground" (v. 17b).

The Dream Game turned into the Wildest-Dream-Come-True Game for Patrick Sparks.

UK wasn't interested in Sparks when his high school playing days ended in 2001, so he wound up at Western Kentucky. After his sophomore season, he looked around for a bigger stage. This time, UK head coach Tubby Smith got it right, and Sparks started for Kentucky from 2004-06.

When the 5-1 Cats took on the Louisville Cardinals on Dec. 18, 2004, in the annual bloodletting that has become known as The Dream Game, Sparks was the Cats' second-leading scorer and the assist leader. After the game, he was also the squad's "undisputed king of clutch" as his every childhood dream came true.

The Cardinals led by ten with 7:30 to play, but Sparks suddenly went on a rampage. He hit three straight treys and then added an old-fashioned three-point play to make it a 54-50 game.

Louisville led 58-57 with 4.8 seconds left, but Kentucky had the ball out of bounds. The pass went into wingman Kelenna Azubuike, who was double-teamed. He dumped a pass to Sparks in the corner, and he let fly, initiating contact with a Cardinal and selling the foul by crashing to the floor.

The refs huddled to determine how much time to put on the

clock, in effect icing Sparks. He paced around the foul line, and his teammates would have nothing to do with him. "Kind of like when a pitcher has a no-hitter going," Sparks said. "Nobody wants to be around him. . . . I was just ready to knock 'em down and get out of here."

He did just that after the officials decided on 0.6 seconds. Three shots. Three points. UK won 60-58. "When you think about how it turned out, it's just crazy," Sparks said. Or a dream come true.

No matter how tightly or doggedly we may cling to our dreams, devotion to them won't make them a reality. Moreover, the cold truth is that all too often dreams don't come true even when we put forth a mighty effort. The realization of our dreams generally results from a head-on collision of persistence and timing.

But what if our dreams don't come true because they're not the same dreams God has for us? That is, they're not good enough and, in many cases, they're not big enough.

God calls us to great achievements because God's dreams for us are greater than our dreams for ourselves. Could the Israelites, wallowing in the misery of slavery, even dream of a land of their own? Could they imagine actually going to such a place?

The fulfillment of such great dreams occurs only when our dreams and God's will for our lives are the same. Our dreams should be worthy of our best — and worthy of God's involvement in making them come true.

It's truly a Cinderella story.
— Patrick Sparks after the 2004 Louisville game

If our dreams are to come true, they must be
worthy of God's involvement in them.

BE KIND

Read Ephesians 4:17-32.

"Be kind and compassionate to one another, forgiving each other, just as in Christ God forgave you" (v. 32).

One lie destroyed Dwane Casey's coaching career. A few small acts of kindness restored it.

Casey lettered four times (1975-79) as a reserve guard at UK. Determined to be a coach, he was a Kentucky graduate assistant during the 1979-80 season.

A Japanese coach named Motoka Kohoma spent the season with the team, studying to become a better coach. He even lived for a time in the players' dormitory. Casey's heart went out to the lonely man. "I was just reaching out to someone who seemed like he needed a friend," he said. Casey gave him rides to practice, ate meals with him, and helped him understand the terminology and the techniques at practice.

Casey was on Eddie Sutton's staff at UK in 1988 when his world crashed around him. An Emery air freight employee claimed to have found an envelope with cash in it addressed from Casey to a recruit. In the wake of the accusation, the entire UK staff resigned after the 1988-89 season, and Casey was put on five years probation, his dreams of coaching apparently shattered forever.

He was sitting at home one evening in 1990 — "not knowing which way I was going to go" — when he received a phone call. It was Kohoma, who remembered Casey's kindness toward him and now returned the favor in a huge way. He offered Casey a coaching job in Japan.

Ultimately, Casey won a lawsuit against Emery, and the NCAA ended his probation. He was exonerated. In 2005, he was named head coach of the Minnesota Timberwolves. In June 2011, he took the head job with the Toronto Raptors.

"It was a blessing for me," Casey said of his time in Japan that got him back into coaching. It resulted from the blessings he had bestowed through his kindness to a lonely man far from home.

We may all talk about kindness, but moving beyond the talk to demonstrating kindness to others is so exceptional in our world that we take notice of it. Witness Motoka Kohoma's remembering how kind Dwayne Casey had been to him. The person who finds a wallet with cash in it and returns it to the owner merits a spot on the evening news. So does the wealthy person who gives a big chunk of change to a hospital or a charity.

Practicing kindness is difficult because it requires us to move beyond our own selves to an awareness of the needs of others and a willingness to do something about those needs without any expectation of blessings in return. A kind person places others first. In an impersonal world, a kind person goes to the time and the trouble to establish personal contact — just as Jesus did and just as God did when he sent Jesus to us.

They were just small acts of kindness.
— *Dwane Casey on Motoka Kohoma*

**Practicing kindness is hard because
it requires us to place others first,
exactly the way Jesus lived among us.**

DAY 22

FIREPROOF

Read Malachi 3:1-5.

"Who can endure the day of his coming? Who can stand when he appears? For he will be like a refiner's fire or a launderer's soap. He will sit as a refiner and purifier of silver" (vv. 2, 3a).

All of a sudden, there was an explosion."

Harold Dennis was 14 years old that horrible day in 1988 when a drunk driver ploughed into his church bus, piercing the fuel tank and bursting the bus into flames. Dennis desperately tried to escape through his window, but it wouldn't budge. When flames filled the front of the bus, the only escape route left was the rear, down the aisle. But panicked children and adults swarmed into that aisle, "their bodies piling up." Harold Dennis was trapped.

He blacked out and never did know how he made it out that rear exit, but somehow he did. "I feel like God took me in his hands," he said, "and carried me back there."

Twenty-seven people, many of them children, died that awful day in the worst drunk-driving accident in U.S. history. Dennis was not among them. Badly burned, he was flown to a Louisville children's hospital. When he charmed a nurse into handing him a mirror, he screamed in horror at what he saw.

His face badly disfigured, Dennis had both the courage and the faith to go on. He walked on to the Kentucky football team as a kicker in 1994. The coaches saw his speed and moved him

WILDCATS

to wide receiver in 1995. He played in eighteen games, caught five passes, returned ten kickoffs, and lettered twice. He received national awards for courage, and his story was made into a movie.

"I never thought I was doing anything special," Dennis said, but head football coach Bill Curry differed. "Harold has already done something special," he said. "He has inspired a state."

The vast majority of us never face the horror and agony of literal fire such as Harold Dennis did. For most of us, fire conjures up images of romantic evenings before a fireplace, fond memories of hot dogs, marshmallows, and ghost stories around a campfire, or rib eyes sizzling on a grill. Fire is an absolutely necessary tool.

Yet we appreciate that fire also has the capacity to destroy. The Bible reflects fire's dual nature, using it to describe almighty God himself and as a metaphor for both punishment and purification. God appeared to Moses in a burning bush and led the wandering Israelites by night as a pillar of fire. Malachi describes Jesus as a purifying and refining fire. Fire is also the ultimate symbol for the destructive force of God's wrath, a side to God we quite understandably prefer not to dwell upon. Our sin and disobedience, though, do not only break God's heart but also anger him.

Thus, fire in the Bible is basically a symbol for God's holiness. Whether that holiness destroys us or purifies us is the choice we make in our response to Jesus. We are, all of us, tested by fire.

God allowed this to happen to me, so I would be able to let people hear my story and maybe change or save a life.
— Harold Dennis

God's holy fire is either the total destroyer or the ultimate purifier; we are fireproof only in Jesus.

THE ANSWER

Read Colossians 2:2-10.

"My purpose is that they . . . may know the mystery of God, namely, Christ, in whom are hidden all the treasures of wisdom and knowledge" (vv. 2, 3).

Kentucky coach Joe B. Hall never forgot the answer he received one night to a routine question he asked a recruit.

In 1968, head coach Adolph Rupp and Hall, an assistant coach at the time, made a recruiting trip to Indiana. Their itinerary called for them to stop first in Marion to catch Greg Starrick in action, then drive to Benton after the first quarter to watch part of a game that featured future Georgia Tech star Rich Younkas, and then return to Marion for a postgame meeting with the Starrick family.

Rupp and Hall had seats right next to Starrick's grandmother. Never known for his tact, not long after the tipoff, Rupp barked "loud enough for everyone within six rows to hear" that he had forgotten his glasses. He then asked Hall which of the players was Starrick, only he used a rather unflattering reference that has to do with the nature of a birth.

Hall remembered that he was "only too glad to escape Grandma's glare" and hit the road to Benton. They also didn't linger because Starrick missed every shot he took in the first quarter.

Back in Benton, Hall asked the taciturn senior how the game had turned out. "We won in overtime," Starrick replied. Hall kept the conversation going by asking, "Did you have a good game?"

"Yes, sir, pretty good," came the reply.

Hall then asked how many points Starrick had scored and got the stunning answer he never forgot. "Eighty-six," Starrick said. He had set a state record with 86 points that night, and Rupp and Hall had not seen a single one of them.

Starrick signed with Kentucky but then transferred to Southern Illinois after his freshman season.

Experience is essentially the uncovering of answers to some of life's questions, both trivial and profound. You often discover to your dismay that as soon as you learn a few answers, the questions change. Your children get older, your health worsens, your financial situation changes, UK's basketball team struggles — all situations requiring answers to a new set of difficulties.

No answers, though, are more important than the ones you seek in your search for God and the meaning of life because they determine your fate for all eternity. Since a life of faith is a journey and not a destination, the questions do indeed change with your circumstances. The "why" or the "what" you ask God when you're a teenager is vastly different from the quandaries you ponder as an adult.

No matter how you phrase the question, though, the answer inevitably centers on Jesus. And that answer never changes.

When you're a driver and you're struggling in the car, you're looking for God to come out of the sky and give you a magical answer.
— NASCAR's Rusty Wallace

It doesn't matter what the question is;
if it has to do with life, temporal or eternal,
the answer lies in Jesus.

DAY 24

UNBELIEVABLE!

Read Hebrews 3:7-19.

"See to it, brothers, that none of you has a sinful, unbelieving heart that turns away from the living God" (v. 12).

The most unbelievable shot in UK basketball history wasn't just a wing-and-a-prayer chunk. Instead, Coach Adolph Rupp gave careful instructions on just how the shot could be made.

Vernon Hatton was All-America as a senior in 1958. He scored 30 points in the NCAA finals to lead the Wildcats to an 84-72 win over Seattle and their fourth national title. Hatton became an instant UK legend, however, not for his performance in the championship game but for his unbelievable shot in what otherwise was an insignificant regular season game.

On Dec. 7, 1957, the 2-0 Wildcats hosted Temple, a team they would meet again in the Final Four. Regulation play ended in a 65-65 tie. Two free throws from Hatton with 49 seconds left forged a tie at 69 in the OT. When a Temple guard hit a short jumper with only three seconds left, though, the Owls had the game in the bag. Or so it seemed.

The Wildcats got the ball to midcourt and then called a time out with only one second left. When play resumed, junior forward John Crigler tossed the ball in to Hatton, who was about a step in front of the midcourt line. He immediately let fly with a set shot that arched toward the basket 47 feet away as the buzzer sounded.

It hit nothing but net. Needless to say, the Kentucky crowd lapsed into complete insanity.

The game required a third overtime before UK won it 85-83.

Perhaps as unbelievable as Hatton's shot was that Rupp carefully set it up. During the time out, he designated Hatton to take the half-court shot and then instructed him to set his feet toward the basket before he caught the ball so he could shoot immediately and without turning any part of his body.

Much of what taxes the limits of our belief system has little direct effect on our lives. Maybe we don't believe in UFOs, honest politicians, aluminum baseball bats, Sasquatch, or the viability of electric cars. A healthy dose of skepticism is a natural defense mechanism that helps protect us in a world that all too often has designs on taking advantage of us.

That's not the case, however, when Jesus and God are part of the mix. Quite unbelievably, we often hear people blithely assert they don't believe in God. Or brazenly declare they believe in God but don't believe Jesus was anything but a good man and a great teacher.

At this point, unbelief becomes dangerous because God doesn't fool around with scoffers. He locks them out of the Promised Land, which isn't a country in the Middle East but Heaven itself.

Given that scenario, it's downright unbelievable that anyone would not believe

I could see it was dead-on perfect all the way.
— UK senior center Ed Beck on Vernon Hatton's unbelievable shot

Perhaps nothing is as unbelievable as that some people insist on not believing in God or his son.

DAY 25

PRESSURE POINT

Read 1 Kings 18:16-40.

"Answer me, O Lord, answer me, so these people will know that you, O Lord, are God" (v. 37).

Even if the players say it doesn't exist, every fan tells them, 'You've got to win [them] all,'" said head coach Rick Pitino. "It" is the pressure of playing basketball at the University of Kentucky.

For the 1995-96 season, Pitino used the invisible beast in the center of Rupp Arena to his team's advantage by playing what was called "a masterful, drawn-out trick of psychology." "I tried to use pressure as a motivational force for my staff and my players," he said. He became a spinmeister of the first order.

For instance, he took the pressure off his players by declaring, "The SEC is too good for us to think of a 16-0 mark." So the team promptly went 16-0 in league play. After the Cats were upset by Mississippi State in the SEC Tournament, Pitino blithely declared, "I was glad we lost" because now the team could turn its attention to what really mattered: the NCAA Tournament.

Pitino even turned his and his players' most overbearing shortcoming into a joke he related all season long. He told of meeting the Pope during the Wildcats' trip to Italy the summer before the 1995-96 season. He kissed the Pope's ring, and the Pope sought to return the favor and remarked, "Oh, you don't have a ring."

As usual, though, the expectations were that come April they would all have one. When one preseason publication rated UK

No. 2, several fans called to ask why they ranked the team so low.

The season unfolded almost perfectly, right on through the 76-67 defeat of Syracuse for the national title. The Orange put the pressure on, twice drawing to within two points in the second half, but each time the Cats responded coolly by stretching their lead.

Pitino said this team would always be known as The Untouchables. Assistant coach Winston Bennett explained, "With all the pressure placed on these guys, they never let any of it touch them."

Like the Wildcats, you live every day with pressure. As Elijah did so long ago, you lay it on the line with everybody watching. Your family, coworkers, or employees — they depend on you. You know the pressure of a deadline, of a job evaluation, of asking someone to go out with you, of driving in rush-hour traffic.

Help in dealing with daily pressure is readily available, and the only price you pay for it is your willingness to believe. God will give you the grace to persevere if you ask prayerfully.

And while you may need some convincing, the pressures of daily living are really small potatoes since they all will pass. The real pressure comes when you stare into the face of eternity because what you do with it is irrevocable and forever. You can handle that pressure easily enough by deciding for Jesus. Eternity is then taken care of; the pressure's off — forever.

The only pressure you've got is good pressure — the type that makes you run faster, jump higher and defend better.
— Rick Pitino to the 1995-96 national champions

The greatest pressure you face in life concerns
where you will spend eternity,
which can be dealt with by deciding for Jesus.

AS A RULE

Read Luke 5:27-32.

"Why do you eat and drink with tax collectors and 'sinners'?" (v. 30b)

Kentucky State College (later known as the University of Kentucky) once flagrantly violated the rules of eligibility in an effort to win a football game. It didn't help.

As the 19th century ended, many colleges routinely used professional players, and "State was one of the worst offenders." As far back as 1894, the school hired W.P Finney, a tackle from Purdue, as the team trainer so he could play against Centre. He showed up, though, on crutches, having broken a leg in a previous game.

Convinced that Kentucky University (today's Transylvania University) had a bunch of ringers for the Thanksgiving matchup of 1903, State officials sent a delegation up the East Coast to scout out and hire some players from other colleges and from athletic clubs. The team State eventually fielded had only a few students from the school while KU used its own players.

Nevertheless, State was totally outclassed and lost 17-0. Only at the end of the game did the State coach put in his "real" players.

In 1904, the chairman of KU's athletic committee obviously remembered the ringers State had brought in the season before. The week of the season-ending game he sent a letter to a member of the State athletic committee that said, in part:

"You may bring your team as you did last year from the four

WILDCATS

quarters of the earth — bring Hottentots, Indians, Patagonans, native Australians, New Yorkers, Danvillans, Whatnots, Topknots — gather them from all the tribes and kindreds of the earth — the more motley the conglomeration the merrier it will be — and we will play you."

Relying on its own students this time, State won 21-4.

Like UK and its relationship with the NCAA, you live by rules that others set up. Some lender determined the interest rate on your mortgage and your car loan. You work hours and shifts somebody else established. Someone else decided what day your garbage gets picked up and what school district your house is in.

Jesus encountered societal rules also, including a strict set of religious edicts that dictated what company he should keep, what people, in other words, were fit for him to socialize with, talk to, or share a meal with. Jesus ignored the rules, choosing love instead of mindless obedience and demonstrating his disdain for society's rules by mingling with the outcasts, the lowlifes, the poor, and the misfits.

You, too, have to choose when you find yourself in the presence of someone whom society deems undesirable. Will you choose the rules or love? Are you willing to be a rebel for love — as Jesus was for you?

[Hiring players] has a bad effect on the student body, tending to encourage insubordination.
— Kentucky State Board of Trustees report after 1903 season

Society's rules dictate who is acceptable
and who is not, but love in the name of Jesus
knows no such distinctions.

MAKING UP

Read Matthew 5:21-24.

"If you . . . remember that your brother has something
against you, leave your gift there in front of the altar. First
go and be reconciled to your brother" (vv. 23-24).

Folks in Lexington were so upset that one fan even suggested
the Ohio River be rerouted to detach Mason County from the rest
of the state. Then Darius Miller made it possible for everyone to
kiss and make up.

As writer Mark Story put it, Miller's "basketball-mad home,
Mason County [and Maysville], had seen its feelings hurt by UK"
in 2004 when it didn't offer a scholarship to one of its own. The
player subsequently starred at Tennessee.

To celebrate that success and perhaps to thumb its nose at UK,
in 2006 Maysville held a special day. Tennessee's head coach was
a guest speaker. When he entered the Mason County gym, the
school's pep band lit into "Rocky Top."

That didn't sit too well with many of the Wildcat faithful.
And, yes, there was at least one call to a Lexington radio station
proposing a massive water project that would separate the rest of
Kentucky from the contamination that was Mason County.

Then along came Miller. After his 2008 senior season at Mason
Co. High, he signed with Kentucky. He played four seasons in
Lexington, including all forty games of the 2011-12 national
championship year. He wound up playing in more games for UK

than anyone else, topping Wayne Turner's previous record by one game with 152. He is the only player from Kentucky to have been named the state's "Mr. Basketball," win a high school state championship, and win a national championship at UK.

He also inadvertently "carried the status of [a] one-man peace delegation between his state university and his hoops-loving hometown." Miller's success in Lexington healed the lingering ill will that had followed Kentucky's earlier snub.

College sports just wouldn't be as much fun if we didn't have rivalries with teams we love to insult, rail against, and whip the daylights out of such as Tennessee. Our personal relationships are totally different, however, though sometimes a spirited disagreement with someone we love is worth it because the kissing and making up is so much fun.

Making up carries an inherent problem, however, because for that reconciliation to occur, somebody must make the first move, which is always the hardest one. So often relationships in our lives are fractured simply because no one has the courage to be the first to attempt to make things right. We hide behind our wounded pride or injured feelings and allow a priceless relationship to wither and die.

The model in such a situation is Jesus. He not only told us to offer a hand and a hug, he lived it, surrendering his life so we could all get right with God.

You might say time and Darius [Miller] have healed those wounds.
— Mason County High principal Steve Appelman

Reconciliation takes courage; just ask Jesus,
who died to get you right with God.

DAY 28

REDEEMED

Read 1 Peter 1:17-25.

"It was not with perishable things such as silver or gold that you were redeemed from the empty way of life handed down to you from your forefathers, but with the precious blood of Christ" (vv. 18-19).

Gerald Fitch badly needed some redemption. A game-winning shot took care of it.

A sophomore guard, Fitch was barely out of head coach Tubby Smith's doghouse when the Cats met Florida on Senior Day 2002. He hadn't played in two weeks, having been put in the unusual position of being suspended by the coach not once but twice.

He was back on the team, though, when UK hosted Florida on March 2 with a share of the SEC's Eastern Division title and a first-round bye in the league tournament at stake. The game was close practically all the way; the biggest difference after the 11-minute mark of the first half was eight points.

Florida led 65-63 when Cliff Hawkins, once referred to as "the player opposing defenses invite to shoot," nailed a 12-foot jumper with 1:37 left to play. "I think when the time comes to make plays, I'm capable of making plays," Hawkins said.

The Gators hit two free throws to lead 67-65, and after a pair of missed charity shots and a turnover, the Cats gathered for a time-out with 39.8 seconds left. The astute betting man would have placed everything on Smith's calling on senior Tayshaun Prince,

WILDCATS

the reigning SEC Player of the Year. He would have lost.

Instead, Smith turned to Fitch, who admitted he was surprised by the call, but was "at the same time, happy and anxious." "He did it at Tennessee. He'd done it about three times this year when we needed threes," the head coach explained.

Fitch made this one too, hitting the trey with 33 seconds left. When Florida didn't score again, the shot was the game-winner in the 70-67 victory. Fitch had his redemption.

In our capitalistic society, we know all about redemption. Just think "rebate" or store or product coupons. To receive the rebates or the discount, though, we must redeem them, cash them in.

"Redemption" is a business term; it reconciles a debt, restoring one party to favor by making amends as was the case with Gerald Fitch after his suspensions. In the Bible, a slave could obtain his freedom only upon the paying of money by a redeemer. In other words, redemption involves the cancelling of a debt the individual cannot pay on his own.

While literal, physical slavery is incomprehensible to us today, we nevertheless live much like slaves in our relationship to sin. On our own, we cannot escape from its consequence, which is death. We need a redeemer, someone to pay the debt that gives us the forgiveness from sin we cannot give ourselves.

We have such a redeemer. He is Jesus Christ, who paid our debt not with money, but with his own blood.

I told myself when I came back, I wanted to do something big.
— Gerald Fitch on coming back from his suspension

To accept Jesus Christ as your savior is to believe his death was a selfless act of redemption.

FACING THE MUSIC

Read Psalm 98.

"Sing to the Lord a new song, for he has done marvelous things" (v. 1).

When Antonio Hall came to Lexington on a recruiting trip, he naturally wanted to check out the football facilities. First, though, he visited the School of Fine Arts.

Hall was one of the most sought-after offensive linemen in the country when he came south from Canton, Ohio, in January 2000 to visit the UK campus. He went on to have an All-SEC career in Lexington. He was a four-year starter at tackle, a Freshman All-America, and was named "Mr. Wildcat," an award presented to the top male student-athlete at the university.

As that latter honor indicates, there was much more to Hall than just size (6-foot-5, 302 lbs.) and his ferocity on the football field. It could be argued that he was, in fact, a musician who just happened to play football.

Doubters need only look back to that initial recruiting trip when Hall met with members of the music faculty before he visited with the football coaches. He didn't just stop by as a courtesy either. He spent almost two hours discussing UK's music program with the faculty. Only then did he turn his attention to football.

Once he was satisfied on both fronts, Hall committed to Kentucky. As *Sports Illustrated* put it, "It's hard to tell who is happier that he did: [renowned tenor and professor Everett] McCorvey [of the music staff], who [was] Hall's voice professor, or football coach Guy Morriss."

Hall is "a Renaissance man" equally at home pounding the piano keys or pounding defensive linemen. He is also a gifted singer who can belt out some opera or lay down a show tune. He got his musical start as a child with the Shiloh Baptist Church choir when he was 4 years old. By the time he was a sophomore in high school, he knew he wanted to study music, so he took up the piano.

And, just for the fun of it, football.

Maybe you have absolutely no rhythm and can't play a lick or carry a tune in the proverbial bucket. Or perhaps you know your way around a guitar or a keyboard and can croon "My Old Kentucky Home" on karaoke night without closing the joint down.

Unless you're a professional musician, however, how well you play or sing really doesn't matter. What counts is that you have music in your heart and sometimes you have to turn it loose.

Worshipping God has always included music in some form. That same boisterous and musical enthusiasm you exhibit when the Basketball Pep Band sounds off in Rupp Arena should be a part of the joy you have in your personal worship of God.

When you consider that God loves you, he always will, and he has arranged through Jesus for you to spend eternity with him, how can that song God put in your heart not burst forth?

I could tell right off that [Antonio Hall] was a very special kid.
— *UK voice professor Everett McCorvey*

You call it music; others may call it noise;
sent God's way, it's called praise.

PROMISES, PROMISES

Read 2 Corinthians 1:16-20.

"No matter how many promises God has made, they are 'Yes' in Christ" (v. 20).

Adolph Rupp kept a promise, and so Kentucky had a new single-game scoring leader.

Dan Issel is a Kentucky legend, a two-time All-America whose 2,138 career points and career average of 25.8 points per game still stand as Wildcat records.

During Issel's junior season of 1968-69, the players were up in arms over the rigorous running program instituted by assistant coach Joe B. Hall. The seniors asked Issel, as the team's star and leader, to talk to Rupp about making it easier on them. Issel had a discussion with his head coach, and Rupp made him an offer he couldn't refuse. He told Issel that if he ran, he would do what he could to get him the single-game record. Issel ran.

The record belonged to Cliff Hagan, who had scored 51 against Temple in 1953. The notion that Issel could break it wasn't exactly far-fetched. After all, he had scored 41 against Vanderbilt and 36 points (with 29 rebounds) against LSU his junior season.

On the night of Feb. 7, 1970, against Ole Miss, Issel had Cotton Nash's career scoring record of 1,770 points squarely in his sights. "I had to have another 40-point game to break the record," he recalled. He didn't know how many points he was scoring as the game went along, but he knew he was having a good night. "It seemed like everything was going in," he said.

The game was a rout as UK led 56-28 at the break. As was his practice, reasonably early in the last half Rupp took Issel and the other starters out to let some of the other guys play. The manager, Doug Billups, noticed that Issel was close to Hagan's record. He told Rupp.

Honoring his promise, the coach put Issel back in, and he set the record with 53 points (broken in 2009 by Jodie Meeks' 54).

The promises you make don't say much about you; the promises you keep tell everything.

The promise to your daughter to be there for her softball game. To your son to help him with his math homework. To your parents to come see them soon. To your spouse to remain faithful until death parts you. And remember what you promised God?

You may carelessly throw promises around, but you can never outpromise God, who is downright profligate with his promises. For instance, he has promised to love you always, to forgive you no matter what you do, and to prepare a place for you with him in Heaven.

And there's more good news in that God operates on this simple premise: Promises made are promises kept. You can rely absolutely on God's promises. The people to whom you make them should be able to rely just as surely on your promises.

[Coach Rupp] said he was a little sorry to see Cliff's record be broken, but that if he didn't want me to do it, he wouldn't have put me back in.
— Dan Issel

**God keeps his promises just as those
who rely on you expect you to keep yours.**

CONFIDENCE MAN

Read Micah 7:5-7.

"As for me, I will look to the Lord, I will wait for the God of my salvation" (v. 7 NRSV).

Entering the 1978 national championship game against Duke, the Cats had something going for them they had not had three seasons before: confidence.

Prior to the 1975 title game against UCLA, Kentucky had the edge. "To a man," said senior All-American forward Kevin Grevey, "the Cats were more talented." "The national championship was within reach."

The day before the title game, however, UCLA head coach John Wooden took the wind out of the Cats' sails: He announced his retirement. UK head coach Joe B. Hall "immediately told us this wasn't going to make a difference in the game," Grevey said, but everyone knew differently. There was simply no way the Bruins would let their legendary coach go out a loser.

They didn't. UCLA won 92-85. Thirty years later, Grevey said, "I've held a grudge against John Wooden all these years. I'll never forget it."

Three seasons later, Kentucky was back in the title game. This time, nothing could shake the Cats' confidence. "The first thing I remember about that game," recalled national Player of the Year Jack "Goose" Givens, "was that before it even started, there was a confidence and a comfort level that I had going into it. It was something different than I had felt in any other game."

A slow start did nothing to shake that team confidence. "We never lost that confidence," Givens said. "We always felt like we were in control."

At halftime, the only anxiety was over how quickly they could get back on the court and finish Duke off. They did just that, confidently winning the national title 94-88.

Givins was the most confident player on the floor that night. He scored 41 points, the third-most ever for the title game.

You need confidence in all areas of your life. You're confident the company you work for will pay you on time, or you wouldn't go to work. You turn the ignition confident your car will start. When you flip a switch, you expect the light to come on.

Confidence in other people and in things is often misplaced, though. Companies go broke; car batteries die; light bulbs burn out. Even the people you love the most sometimes let you down.

So where can you place your trust with absolute confidence you won't be betrayed? In the promises of God.

Such confidence is easy, of course, when everything's going your way, but what about when you cry as Micah did, "What misery is mine!" As Micah declares, that's when your confidence in God must be its strongest. That's when you wait for the Lord confident that God will not fail you, that he will never let you down.

We felt we were the better team, and we were confident.
— Jack Givins on the 1978 national championship game

People, things, and organizations will let you down; only God can be trusted confidently.

FATHER FIGURE

Read Luke 3:1-22.

"And a voice came from heaven: 'You are my Son, whom I love; with you I am well pleased'" (v. 22).

Trying to make the UK basketball team as a walk-on was interfering with Todd Svoboda's first priority: academics. Thus, he considered quitting, but before he decided, he called his dad.

A chemical engineering major, Svoboda transferred to Kentucky in 1992 after three seasons as a star at Northern Kentucky. With one year of eligibility left, he decided to walk onto a Wildcat team that included All-American Jamal Mashburn, All-SEC point guard Travis Ford, and the nation's No. 1 recruiting class.

Svoboda soon realized "the magnitude of the time and energy needed to balance a basketball career at Kentucky with a major in chemical engineering." He considered quitting and called his father, who had been through the same grind as a chemical-engineering major and varsity tennis player at Purdue.

Dad had some good advice; he told his son he would regret it if he quit, that years later he didn't want to look back and wonder if he could have made it had he kept going. So Svoboda stayed, made the team, and had one of the great moments of his life.

He played 38 minutes in 13 games during the sensational 30-4 season of 1992-93. As the Cats blew out FSU in the finals of the Southeast Regional, Svoboda got in. With the last seconds ticking away, he put up a three and hit it. The whole bench jumped off the ground. "They were cheering for me, for hitting that shot. That's what makes it all worthwhile," he said.

Years later he still had an old newspaper photo that showed him shooting the three and in the background every player on the bench cheering him on. "And I still have my piece of net," he said. All because he followed some advice from his father.

Contemporary American society largely belittles and marginalizes fathers and their influence upon their sons. Men are perceived as necessary to effect pregnancy; after that, they can leave and everybody's better off.

But we need look in only two places to appreciate the enormity of that misconception: our jails — packed with males who lacked the influence of fathers in their lives as they grew up — and the Bible. God — being God — could have chosen any relationship he desired between Jesus and himself, including society's approach of irrelevancy.

Instead, the most important relationship in all of history was that of father-son. God obviously believes a close, loving relationship between fathers and sons — like that between Todd Svoboda and his dad — is crucial. For men and women to espouse otherwise or for men to walk blithely and carelessly out of their children's lives constitutes disobedience to the divine will.

Simply put, God loves fathers. After all, he is one.

It's something I can always tell my kids and my grandkids.
— Todd Svoboda on hitting the trey in the NCAA Tournament

Fatherhood is a tough job, but a model
for the father-child relationship is found
in that of Jesus the Son with God the Father.

PLAN AHEAD

Read Psalm 33:1-15.

"The plans of the Lord stand firm forever, the purposes of his heart through all generations" (v. 11).

Unbeknown to their coach, some Kentucky football players had a plan to remedy an injustice.

W.C. Harrison, who lettered from 1910-12, played every minute of all ten games in 1912 and captained both the football and the basketball teams that year. On the train ride to Knoxville for the Tennessee game of Nov. 16, Harrison complained that in all the time he had played football, he had never scored a touchdown, not exactly an unusual situation for a tackle. Joking around, several of Harrison's teammates told him they would remedy that situation the next day.

As the miles and the talk rolled on, though, the players decided to make good on their joke. Starting center J.S. "Brick" Chambers and William "Red Doc" Rodes, who played defensive end alongside Harrison, were the leaders in the plot. They determined that the best way for the left tackle to score a touchdown would be on a blocked kick. They carefully drew up their plans.

Chambers would break through the line and take out the Vol blocking back protecting the kicker. Rodes had to get in and block the kick, leaving Harrison free to pick up the loose ball and run for glory. And the goal line.

Their plan worked to perfection; Harrison romped 20 yards

with the blocked kick for the first touchdown. It turned out to be a big play as Kentucky won 13-6. After the game, the ball was given to Harrison to commemorate the only touchdown he ever scored.

Following a prosperous career as a farmer and the owner of a rolling mill, Harrison entered the ministry. He eventually taught at a Bible college in South America with his prized football making the trip with him. In 1939, he sent the ball back to Lexington to the athletic department as part of a project researching the early days of Kentucky football.

Successful living takes planning. You go to school to improve your chances for a better paying job. You use blueprints to build your home. You plan for retirement. You map out your vacation to have the best time. You even plan your children — sometimes.

Your best-laid plans, however, sometime get wrecked by events and circumstances beyond your control. The economy goes into the tank; a debilitating illness strikes; a hurricane hits. Life is capricious and thus no plans — not even your best ones — are foolproof.

But you don't have to go it alone. God has plans for your life that guarantee success as God defines it if you will make him your planning partner. God's plan for your life includes joy, love, peace, kindness, gentleness, and faithfulness, all the elements necessary for truly successful living for today and for all eternity. And God's plan will not fail.

A man without a plan doesn't have a future.
— TCU head football coach Gary Patterson

Your plans may ensure a successful life;
God's plans will ensure a successful eternity.

DAY 34

REGRETS, ANYONE?

Read 2 Corinthians 7:8-13.

"Godly sorrow brings repentance that leads to salvation and leaves no regret" (v. 10).

Alex Meyer walked away from $2 million — and had no regrets.

Coming out of high school in 2008 as Indiana's Player of the Year, Meyer, a 6-foot-9 right-handed pitcher, was drafted in the 20th round by the Boston Red Sox. Knowing Meyer was considering college, the Sox offered him $2.2 million to sign. He turned them down, opting instead to head south to Lexington to pitch for the Wildcats.

Meyer had his reasons for deciding against enough money to set him up for life. For one thing, college, not professional baseball, was the most important thing in his life at the time. With a remarkably mature perspective for one so young, he also said he "needed to get stronger and mentally mature and if that were to happen, it would benefit me more, I felt, than signing."

So he left the money on the table and came to Kentucky to pitch for free — or at least for the benefits of a scholarship. Again, his decision was carefully made. He chose UK because he wanted to play in the country's best college baseball conference and it was close enough to home to allow his family to come to the games.

He did very well, topping off his career with a junior season in 2011 that saw him named All-SEC. He went 7-5 and led the Cats in starts, wins, ERA (2.94), innings pitched, and strikeouts. His

110 K's led the SEC and was ninth nationally. He was twice the SEC Pitcher of the Week and once the National Player of the Week.

But that success took three years. Did he have any regrets about walking away from all that money? "It was the best decision I've made in my life," Meyer said as his junior season wound down.

Any momentary lapses into regret were resolved for good when the Washington Nationals drafted Meyer in the first round of the 2011 draft, making him the highest pick in UK history. In August he signed a pro contract that included a $2 million signing bonus.

In their classic hit "The Class of '57," the Statler Brothers served up some pure country truth when they sang, "Things get complicated when you get past 18." That complication includes regrets; you have them; so does everyone else: situations and relationships that upon reflection we wish we had handled differently.

Feeling troubled or remorseful over something you've done or left undone is not necessarily a bad thing. That's because God uses regrets to spur us to repentance, which is the decision to change our ways. Repentance in turn is essential to salvation through Jesus Christ. You regret your un-Christlike actions, you repent by promising God to mend your ways, and then you seek and receive forgiveness for them.

The cold, hard truth is that you will have more regrets in your life. You can know absolutely, however, that you will never ever regret making Jesus the reason for that life.

Absolutely, I made the right decision.
— Alex Meyer, with no regrets about choosing college

**Regrets are part of living,
but you'll never regret living for Jesus.**

ANIMAL MAGNETISM

Read Psalm 139:1-18.

"For you created my inmost being; you knit me together in my mother's womb. I praise you because I am fearfully and wonderfully made" (vv. 13-14).

Cadets. Colonels. Corn-Crackers. Thoroughbreds. Finally, however, they became the Wildcats.

In the early days of the school's athletic endeavors, the teams of what was Kentucky State College and then Kentucky State University went by various nicknames, including the first four listed above. In chapel the morning after the 6-2 upset of Illinois on Oct. 9, 1909, (See Devotion No. 59.), the school commandant praised the team by declaring the boys "fought like Wildcats." The name caught on and was officially adopted by the football team in 1911.

During a banquet following the 1920 football season, someone suggested that "a real, honest-to-goodness wild wildcat" would make a good mascot. R.S. Webb, a center for the teams of 1908-10 and an assistant coach in 1911-12, began a search for a suitable cat.

He soon purchased one that was expressed to Lexington from San Antonio, but "Tom" quickly died. "TNT" succeeded to the job, but soon died also. "Whiskers" was the third try at a live mascot, but that cat died during a UK basketball game in 1924. A cat from New Mexico was the next designated mascot.

Other attempts at keeping a live mascot followed, but they, too, failed as the cats died or were released back into the wild because

WILDCATS

they did not thrive in captivity. The last try came in 1969 with "Baby," but a complaint about the way the cat was handled on the sideline ended Baby's career after two games.

The most successful of the live mascots was "Colonel," who served from 1947-54. Sent to the state wildlife farm upon his retirement, he soon contracted pneumonia and died.

Today, Blue, a live bobcat, serves as the mascot though he never attends games because of the innate shyness that limits his interaction with large crowds. He lives at a wildlife center.

Animals such as Blue elicit our awe and our respect. Nothing enlivens a trip more than glimpsing turkeys, deer, or even wildcats in the wild. Admit it: You go along with the kids' trip to the zoo because you think it's a cool place too. All that variety of life is mind-boggling. Who could conceive of a wildcat, a moose, or a prairie dog? Who could possibly have that rich an imagination?

But the next time you're in a crowd, look around at the parade of faces. Who could come up with the idea for all those different people? For that matter, who could conceive of you? You are unique, a masterpiece who will never be duplicated.

The master creator, God Almighty, is behind it all. He thought of you and brought you into being. If you had a manufacturer's label, it might say, "Lovingly, fearfully, and wonderfully handmade in Heaven by #1 — God."

Of battle, [the Wildcat] is not afraid, from difficulty he does not turn aside, and when aroused, other beasts hold no terror for him.
— The Kentuckian

You may consider some painting or a magnificent animal a work of art; the real masterpiece is you.

BELIEVE IT

Read John 3:16-21.

"For God so loved the world that He gave His only begotten Son, that whoever believes in Him should not perish but have everlasting life" (v. 16 NKJV).

The roof caved in; the bottom fell out. However it's phrased, times were tough for UK basketball; nevertheless, John Pelphrey and his teammates believed.

Pelphrey and Deron Feldhaus were redshirt freshman in 1987-88 as the Cats raced to a 27-6 record and the Sweet 16. But then the good times came to a screeching halt. NCAA sanctions and the resulting player defections gutted the program. The 1988-89 team went 13-19, and the coach joined the exodus from Lexington.

But not Pelphrey, Feldhaus, and Richie Farmer. "Growing up, I always wanted to play for Kentucky," Pelphrey said. "To be there when the school needed us, we couldn't leave."

In came Rick Pitino, and the three may have wished they had left. He installed a running program to develop his athletes into players who could run and press. Farmer and Pelphrey struggled to run two miles in the required twelve minutes. After weeks of trying, they had one last chance. "John if you belong to a church, say a prayer," strength and conditioning coach Ray "Rock" Oliver told Pelphrey. He made it at 12:00, Farmer at 12:01. Oliver later admitted he didn't have a stop watch.

The "ragtag group" that was the 1989-90 Wildcats had only

eight players, but with a run-and-gun offense that featured the three-pointer and a pressing defense they went a surprising 14-14.

The only game in which they had no chance was the matchup of Feb. 15, 1990, against LSU with a pair of seven-footers and an All-American guard. But as Pelphrey put it, "Sometimes, you just have to believe." They did and they did it, stunning LSU 100-95.

Years later in his coaching career, Pelprey used that LSU game to illustrate to his players what can happen if they only believe.

What we believe underscores everything about our lives. Our politics. How we raise our children. How we treat other people. Whether we respect others, their property and their lives.

Often, competing belief systems clamor for our attention; we all know persons — maybe friends and family members — who have lost Christianity in the shuffle and the hubbub.

We turn aside from believing in Christ at our peril, however, because the heart and soul, the very essence of Christianity, is belief. That is, believing that this man named Jesus is the very Son of God and that it is through him — and only through him — that we can find forgiveness and salvation that will reserve a place for us with God.

But believing is more than simply acknowledging intellectually that Jesus is God. Even the demons who serve Satan know that. It is belief so deep that we entrust our lives and our eternity to Christ. We live like we believe it — because we do.

It was all about believing you could do it, and working hard.
— John Pelphrey on what some called the "miracle" 1989-90 season

Believe it: Jesus is the way — and the only way
— to eternal life with God.

HOLLYWOOD ENDING

Read Luke 24:1-12.

*"Why do you look for the living among the dead? He is
not here; he has risen!" (vv. 5, 6a)*

The script the Cats of 2013-14 used in the NCAA Tournament
stayed the same in the semifinals. It was right out of Hollywood.

The recruiting class John Calipari assembled prior to the season was hailed as the greatest ever. Their collective talent was
exceeded only by the expectations placed upon them.

The season did not go as expected. The youngest lineup in the
country struggled, the team "undone by egos, bad guard play,
and player and coach frustration." The Cats lost ten games and
dropped out of the top 25 at season's end.

That's when Hollywood took over. Calipari said it was something much more mundane than Tinsel Town magic: It simply
took his latest one-and-done model four months to figure it out.

Whatever it was, the Cats wound up as the No. 8 seed in what
was called "the region of death." "Instead of going down as the
great flop of the one-and-done-era," the Kiddie Cats used a script
Hollywood could have come up with to make a magical run all
the way to the national championship game. That script was quite
simple but extremely dramatic: "Hang around in the first half, get
it close by halftime, make a second-half run and then pull out a
heart-stopping victory."

Wisconsin was the opponent in that April 5 semi-final game,

and, sure enough, the Cats trailed at halftime. True to form, though, they rallied and pulled off more Hollywood-style heroics.

Wisconsin took a 73-71 lead with 16.4 seconds left. Aaron Harrison hadn't taken a 3 all game, but he pulled up and nailed a 24-foot, NBA-range shot with 5.7 seconds left. UK had a 74-73 win.

His hands in the air in disbelief, Calipari exclaimed, "Another great game." And another Hollywood ending.

The world tells us that happy endings are for fairy tales and the movies, that reality is Cinderella dying in childbirth and her prince getting killed in a peasant uprising. But that's just another of the world's lies.

The truth is that Jesus Christ has been producing happy endings for almost two millennia. That's because in Jesus lies the power to change and to rescue a life no matter how desperate the situation. Jesus is the master at putting shattered lives back together, of healing broken hearts and broken relationships, of resurrecting lost dreams.

And as for living happily ever after — God really means it. The greatest Hollywood ending of them all was written on a Sunday morning centuries ago when Jesus left a tomb and death behind. With faith in Jesus, your life can have that same ending. You live with God in peace, joy, and love — forever. The End.

This run, these games, these finishes — Hollywood couldn't come up with a script like this.
— Writer Eric Lindsey on UK's run to the championship game in 2014

Hollywood's happy endings are products of imagination; the happy endings Jesus produces are real and are yours for the asking.

DAY 38

OLD-FASHIONED

Read Leviticus 18:1-5.

"You must obey my laws and be careful to follow my decrees. I am the Lord your God" (v. 4).

Erik Daniels was such a throwback kind of player that his Wildcat basketball teammates nicknamed him "Old School."

In 2000-01 and 2001-02, Daniels was a bit player. He started only one game and averaged 13 minutes per contest. He wasn't considered a good shooter, and, in fact, even Daniels admitted that his playing style was "unorthodox." His teammates had other words for it. "Awkward," said Keith Bogans, the 2002-03 SEC Player of the Year. "Tricky," said guard Gerald Fitch with great tact.

In other words, not even Daniels' fellow Wildcats were ready for what happened in 2002-03 when Daniels suddenly broke out to become "one of the most indispensable players on the Southeastern Conference's most dominant basketball team." On a Cat squad that went 32-4 and roared through the SEC undefeated, Daniels' play made him one of the league's most versatile players.

"Erik brings a spark," declared Chuck Hayes, the 2004 SEC Defensive Player of the Year. "You're talking about a power forward who can pass like a point guard," said Fitch. "We feed off him. He's the type of player who makes everybody else better."

And so the players nicknamed Daniels "Old School" because he could do a little bit of everything and do it well: pass, shoot, rebound, and play defense. Head coach Tubby Smith agreed with his players' description of Daniels as "old school," calling him a "throwback player." Daniels wasn't even sure exactly what that meant, but he didn't mind the label.

Even after he broke into the starting lineup his junior season, Daniels commented he would do what he could to help the team, "whether it's starting or being out there on the bench." Spoken like a true old-school player.

Usually, when we refer to some person, idea, or institution as old-fashioned, we deliver a full-fledged or at least thinly veiled insult. They're out of step with the times and the mores, hopelessly out of date, totally irrelevant, and quite useless.

For the people of God, however, "old-fashioned" is exactly the lifestyle we should pursue. The throwbacks are the ones who value honor, dignity, sacrifice, and steadfastness, who can be counted on to tell the truth and to do what they say. Old-fashioned folks shape their lives according to eternal values and truths, the ones handed down by almighty God.

These ancient laws and decrees are still relevant to contemporary life because they direct us to a lifestyle of holiness and righteousness that serves us well every single day. Such a way of living allows us to escape the ultimately hopeless life to which so many have doomed themselves in the name of being modern.

I am a firm believer that if you can't get it the old-fashioned way, you don't need it.
— *Bo Jackson*

The ancient lifestyle God calls us to still leads us to a life of contentment, peace, and joy, which never grows old-fashioned.

DAY 39

THE SIMPLE LIFE

Read 1 John 1:5-10.

*"If we confess our sins, he is faithful and just and
will forgive us our sins and purify us from all
unrighteousness" (v. 9).*

Brandon Knight had a simple formula for winning games in
the NCAA Tournament: Miss most (or all) of your shots except
the last one.

A freshman, Knight started all 38 games at point guard for the
29-9 Kentucky team of 2010-11. He was the team's leading scorer
at 17.3 points per game and the squad's assist leader at 4.2 a night
and led the Cats all the way to the Final Four. Two of the games in
the NCAA Tournament followed what apparently was the Knight
formula for a UK win.

Knight was the kid in the driveway counting down the ticks
on an imaginary clock and waiting until the last second to let fly
with a shot that inevitably won the fictitious game. "He'd dribble
and launch a step-back jumper, then hold his follow-through, posing for dramatic effect."

Those childhood fantasies came true twice in the 2011 drive to
the Final Four, though perhaps Knight never envisioned missing
as many shots as he did on the way to nailing the game-winners.

In the second round of the 2011 NCAA Tournament, Knight
suffered through every shooter's nightmare against Princeton. He
missed every single shot, all seven of them, and had not scored

WILDCATS

a single point as the game ticked down to its final seconds. But then Knight drove through the Princeton defense and scored on a layup with two seconds to play. That was the difference in the 59-57 Wildcat win.

Knight apparently decided to repeat his simple formula in the next game against No.-1 seed Ohio State. He hit only four of his first eleven shots, but then he hit the last one, a 15-foot jumper with 5.4 seconds left that was the difference in the 62-60 win.

Perhaps the simple life in America was doomed by the arrival of the programmable VCR, which itself has been rendered defunct by superior technology. Since then, we've pretty much been on an escalating and downward spiral into ever more complicated lives.

But we might do well in our own lives to keep it simple. That is, we should approach our lives with the keen awareness that success requires simplicity, a sticking to the basics: Revere God, love our families, honor our country, do our best.

Theologians may make what God did in Jesus as complicated as quantum mechanics and the infield fly rule, but God kept it simple for us: believe, trust, and obey. Believe in Jesus as the Son of God, trust that through him God makes possible our deliverance from our sins into Heaven, and obey God in the way he wants us to live.

It's simple, but it's the true winning formula, the way to win for all eternity.

I think he just misses on purpose and tries to hit the game-winner.
— UK guard Doron Lamb on the Knight formula for a win

Life today is complicated, but God made it simple for us when he showed up as Jesus.

DAY 40

YOU DECIDE

Read John 6:60-69.

"The words I have spoken to you are spirit and they are life. Yet there are some of you who do not believe" (vv. 63b-64a).

Because of a bizarre rule, an undefeated UK basketball team decided not to play in the NCAA Tournament.

Led by the Big Three of Cliff Hagan, Frank Ramsey, and Lou Tsioropoulos, the Wildcats of 1953-54 went undefeated, the first Kentucky squad to do so since the team of 1911-12 (9-0). When the regular season ended, both Kentucky and LSU were undefeated in SEC play, a scheduling disagreement having kept them from playing. The two met on March 9 in a playoff game to determine the league champion and a berth in the NCAA Tournament. UK won 63-56 in what Ramsey called "the only close game we played all season" to finish the year 25-0. The tournament and a shot at the national championship was up next.

Or maybe not.

The NCAA declared that Hagan, Ramsey, and Tsioropoulos were ineligible for the tournament because they were no longer undergraduates. Previously, the NCAA had banned Kentucky from playing basketball for the 1952-53 season. The players had to sit out, so they practiced and went to class. Thus, they earned their bachelor's degrees early and were post-graduates at the time. "If we had taken five years to graduate, we wouldn't have had a problem," Ramsey pointed out. "So we were penalized for trying to do the right thing. Isn't that something?"

Exactly what happened has been reported differently over the years, but Tsioropoulos once said that the team voted 9-3 to take part in the tournament without the big three. He spoke up and pointed out that the team would not have won all those games without the big three, who had done most of the scoring. Head coach Adolph Rupp agreed and the team decided to stay home.

LaSalle, a team UK had beaten by 13 points, won the title.

The decisions you have made along the way have shaped your life at every pivotal moment. Some decisions you made suddenly and carelessly; some you made carefully and deliberately; some were forced upon you. You may have discovered that some of those spur-of-the-moment decisions have turned out better than your carefully considered ones.

Of all your life's decisions, however, none is more important than one you cannot ignore: What have you done with Jesus? Even in his time, people chose to follow Jesus or to reject him, and nothing has changed; the decision must still be made and nobody can make it for you. Ignoring Jesus won't work either; that is, in fact, a decision, and neither he nor the consequences of your decision will go away.

Carefully considered or spontaneous — how you arrive at a decision for Jesus doesn't matter; all that matters is that you get there.

There will be no voting because you guys are not going.
— Lou Tsioropoulos to his teammates on the NCAA Tournament

A decision for Jesus may be spontaneous or considered; what counts is that you make it.

DAY 41

YOUNG BLOOD

Read Jeremiah 1:4-10.

*"The Lord said to me, 'Do not say, 'I am only a child' . . .
for I am with you and will rescue you" (vv. 7a, 8).*

Taking the field against SEC competition as a freshman didn't
faze Dennis Johnson. After all, he had played his first high-school
football game when he was 6 years old.

Johnson played defensive end for the Wildcats from 1999-2001,
starting 29 games. He set a school record as a junior in 2001 when
he led the SEC with twelve sacks. He was Third-Team All-America
and First-Team All-SEC that season and then decided to forgo his
senior season and enter the NFL draft.

Johnson started out young for the Cats and matured, but that
was nothing compared to what he did when he was younger. As
strange as it may sound, he was a member of his high school football team when he was in the second grade. And he wasn't the
manager; he saw real live action. He was 6 years old.

The team was coached by Dennis' father, Alvis. Derrick, his
older brother, also played; he was 7 and in the third grade. The
Johnson brothers are believed to be the youngest participants in a
high-school sport in the country's history.

But don't get the impression they were tiny, overmatched little
boys. At the time, Dennis was 5-foot-7 and weighed 170 pounds.
Derrick was even bigger. Their dad recalled that when he put Dennis into his first game (at guard), he told his son to block the line-

WILDCATS

backer. Dennis put the player on the ground. "I'm sure none of the people knew how old the boys were," dad said. "You couldn't tell them from a lot of the other kids." Momma sure knew. When her boys went in, she prayed, "God take care of them and help Alvis make good decisions. But it was fun."

When the Johnsons' story received some publicity, Kentucky adopted a rule that prohibited students from playing on a varsity team until the ninth grade. In his day, though, Dennis wasn't too young to play, no matter how young he was.

While today's media seem inordinately obsessed with youth, most aspects of our society value experience and some hard-won battle scars. Life usually requires us to spend time on the bench as a reserve, waiting for our chance to play with the big boys and girls. Unlike Dennis Johnson, you probably rode some pine in high school. You entered college as a freshman. You stated out in your career at an entry-level position.

Paying your dues is traditional, but that should never stop you from doing something bold and daring right away. Nowhere is this more true than in your faith life.

You may assert that you are too young and too inexperienced to really do anything worthwhile for God. Those are just excuses, however, and God won't pay a lick of attention to them when he issues a call.

After all, the younger you are, the more time you have to serve.

One of the guys on the team had to teach me how to tie my shoes.
 — *Derrick Johnson on playing high-school football in the third grade*

**Youth is no excuse for not serving God;
it just gives you more time.**

KENTUCKY

DAY 42

UNSTOPPABLE

Read Revelation 20.

"Fire came down from heaven and devoured them. And the devil, who deceived them, was thrown into the lake of burning sulfur, where the beast and the false prophet had been thrown" (vv. 9b-10a).

Not even a fire alarm or a time out that eliminated a game-winning basket could stop the UK women from beating Louisville.

Coach Mickie DeMoss and her 3-2 team paired up with the Cardinal women on Dec. 3, 2003, to put on a wild overtime show at Rupp Arena. The Wildcats led by 14 at intermission, only to find themselves behind by ten points with under seven minutes left. They then rallied to force a tie and free basketball.

"That was a weird kind of game with all the lead changes," DeMoss said. But the mood swings weren't the only aspects of the night that were weird.

There's that business about the fire alarm, for instance. After Louisville went up 61-51 with 6:42 left, DeMoss switched her team to a zone defense that keyed an offensive outburst. Soph guard Jenny Pfeiffer buried a pair of threes, and forward Keiko Tate had an old-fashioned three-point play. The lead was down to one when suddenly the arena's fire alarm sounded off.

Tate immediately had a concern, but it had nothing to do with fire. "I was like, 'Please don't let them call off this game,'" she said. After all, she was on her way to a career-high 18 points.

WILDCATS

As it turned out, the hottest thing in the building was the Cat team, so the game soon started up again. With time running out, point guard Angela Phillips hit a layup for what appeared to be a game-winning bucket. But DeMoss had signaled for a time out just before Phillips' shot, and unfortunately a referee saw it.

So after the basket was waved off, the teams went into overtime. Junior Sara Potts (who was twice second-team All-SEC) scored the OT's first five points, and a team that couldn't be stopped on this night no matter what claimed an 84-80 win.

Maybe your unfortunate experience with an unstoppable opponent involved a game against a team full of major college prospects, a league tennis match against a former college player, or your presentation for the project you knew didn't stand a chance. Whatever it was, you've been slam-dunked before.

Being part of an unstoppable team is certainly more fun than being in the way of one. Just ask the Louisville women that night in 2003. Or consider the forces of evil aligned against God. At least the Cardinal players suited up hoping for a win. No such hope exists for those who oppose God.

That's because their fate is already spelled out in detail. It's in the book; we all know how the story ends. God's enemies may talk big and bluster now, but they will be soundly trounced and routed in the most decisive defeat of all time.

You sure want to be on the winning side in that one.

We kept fighting and we didn't give up.
— Keiko Tate on the win over Louisville

The most lopsided victory in all of history is
a sure thing: God's ultimate triumph over evil.

FOOD FOR THOUGHT

Read Genesis 9:1-7.

"Everything that lives and moves will be food for you. Just as I gave you the green plants, I now give you everything" *(v. 3).*

The first seven-footer to play in college had direct instructions from Adolph Rupp about how he could earn a scholarship to Kentucky: Eat.

In 1949-50, Bill Spivey was First-Team All-SEC and Third-Team All America; the following season, he was the National Player of the Year and First-Team All-America as he led the Cats to their third national championship. He averaged 19.2 points per game those two seasons. In the 68-58 win over Kansas State for the '51 national title, he scored 22 points and had 21 rebounds.

Spivey was 6-8 by the time he was in the tenth grade, and his school didn't have any shoes big enough to fit him. He played the year wearing three pairs of sweat socks but drew an inordinate number of walking calls because the socks slid every time he made a move. The next season, he got a pair of size 12 sneakers, which were too small, and cut the toes out with a razor blade. "I got blisters on my toes, but at least I stopped the walking violations," Spivey said. (At Kentucky, Spivey required a handmade extra-long bed that took up most of the dorm room.)

When he came to Rupp's attention, the coach called him "a mess. He was seven feet tall and only weighed 160 or 165 pounds." But

Rupp decided to take a chance — with a condition. He told Spivey if he could gain 40 pounds, he would get a scholarship. "I think I can," Spivey replied. "If I eat regularly and get plenty, I'll make it."

Rupp got Spivey a job in a local drug store where he cleaned the fluorescent ceiling lights without using a ladder. That job allowed assistant coach Harry Lancaster to put their spindly prospect on a special diet. Every day, Spivey drank four malted milks with eggs in them. He gained his 40 pounds and Rupp kept his promise.

Belly up to the buffet, boys and girls, for barbecue and sirloin steak, grilled chicken, and fried catfish with hush puppies and cheese grits. Rachael Ray's a household name; hamburger joints, pizza parlors, and taco stands lurk on every corner; and we have television channels devoted exclusively to food. We love our chow.

Food is one of God's really good ideas, but consider the complex divine plan that begins with a seed and ends with peanuts. The creator of all life devised a system in which living things are sustained and nourished physically through the sacrifice of other living things in a way similar to what Christ underwent to save us spiritually. Whether it's fast food or home-cooked, everything we eat is a gift from God secured through a divine plan in which some plants and animals have given up their lives.

Pausing to give thanks before we dive in seems the least we can do.

I'm convinced he can eat, but can he play basketball?
— Adolph Rupp on Bill Spivey

God created a system that nourishes us
through the sacrifice of other living things;
that's worth a thank-you.

DAY 44

SOMETHING NEW

Read Colossians 3:1-17.

"[S]ince you have taken off your old self with its practices and have put on the new self, which is being renewed in knowledge in the image of its Creator" (vv. 9-10).

In 1891, something new came to the campus of what would become the University of Kentucky: this game called football.

Football as we know it today at UK was born on April 10, 1891, when Kentucky State College (as UK was called then) defeated Georgetown College 8-2. A second game that season ended when a player was knocked unconscious on the first play. He was not seriously injured, but officials decided to stop play.

The first season ended on Dec. 19 with a 10-0 loss to Centre College. A crowd of more than 500 showed up for the game at the Lexington baseball park. The players wore old gray uniforms, cut off at the knee and stuffed with hay for padding, and stockings of various colors borrowed from their sisters or anybody handy.

The reporter covering the game noted that when the State College boys got their first glimpse of the opponent, they "got a little 'skeered at the outset.'" The first half lasted 45 minutes; the last half was called after 20 minutes because of darkness. The game forever established that "football would be a major interest of schools throughout the Bluegrass area."

Football of sorts had been given a try at the school ten years before, but the game actually was more like rugby. Not everyone

WILDCATS

was pleased with it either. In December 1880, a group of students from what was then known as Kentucky A&M College was playing football when a man was upset by all the noise. He fired a pistol at the boys and then chased the students when they ran, "repeatedly load[ing] and fir[ing] when anyone appeared in sight." Eventually, a few of the more daring — or the less judicious — students knocked the gun from his hand and then "they all pitched in and gave him a severe drubbing."

New things in our lives often have a life-changing effect. A new spouse, for instance. A new baby. A new job. A new college sport. Even something as mundane as a new TV set, a lawn mower, or a new hairstyle jolts us with change.

While new experiences, new people, and new toys may make our lives new, they can't make new lives for us. Inside, where it counts — down in the deepest recesses of our soul — we're still the same, no matter how desperately we may wish to change.

An inner restlessness drives us to seek escape from a life that is a monotonous routine. Such a mundane existence just isn't good enough for someone who is a child of God; it can't even be called living. We want more out of life; something's got to change.

The only hope for a new life lies in becoming a brand new man or woman. And that is possible only through Jesus Christ, he who can make all things new again.

The faculty, who have taken little interest in the game, are determined now to encourage the athletic feature of the college.
— Lexington Daily Press *after the 1891 Centre football game*

A brand new you with the promise of a life worth living is waiting in Jesus Christ.

THE UNEXPECTED

Read Matthew 24:36-51.

*"No one knows about that day or hour, not even the
angels in heaven, nor the Son, but only the Father" (v. 36).*

Cameron Mills expected that his would be an unremarkable career at Kentucky. Unexpectedly, it didn't turn out that way.

"I just wanted to play at Kentucky," Mills said. "Even if I rode the bench for four years and never got a chance to play, . . . I just wanted to wear the uniform." So, expecting little or nothing, he walked on in the fall of 1994.

What he got was a full measure of head coach Rick Pitino's disdain. He called Mills the fattest player he had ever seen and once famously said Mills couldn't guard his desk. During the national championship season of 1995-96, Mills played a grand total of sixteen minutes after playing 32 minutes his freshman season.

His junior season of 1996-97 didn't appear to offer anything more than what he expected, though Pitino put him on scholarship. There he was, a walk-on, sitting at the end of the bench and watching everyone else play. Then in January, starting two-guard Derek Anderson tore his ACL; Mills was the only other two-guard on the team. "Really, out of desperation and nowhere else to turn, Coach Petino put me in," Mills said.

What happened was totally unexpected. "I started hitting three pointers, and I kept hitting them,"Mills said. He scored 16 points in the SEC Tournament title game and went on to be the team's second-leading scorer in the '97 NCAA Tournament. During the team practice the day of the national championship game against Arizona, Pitino scolded a player for leaving "the greatest shooter in the country" open. He was speaking of Mills.

Mills, who went into the ministry following his graduation, hit 38 treys for the 1998 national champs as he played in 38 of the 39 games. Unexpectedly, he remains UK's all-time leader in season and career three-point percentages.

Just like Cameron Mills and his Kentucky career, we think we've got everything figured out and under control, and then something unexpected happens. About the only thing we can expect from life with any certainty is the unexpected.

God is that way too, suddenly showing up to remind us he's still around. A friend who calls and tells you he's praying for you, a hug from your child or grandchild, a lone lily that blooms in your yard — unexpected moments when the divine comes crashing into our lives with such clarity that it takes our breath away and brings tears to our eyes.

But why shouldn't God do the unexpected? The only factor limiting what God can do in our lives is the paucity of our own faith. We should expect the unexpected from God, this same deity who caught everyone by surprise by unexpectedly coming to live among us as a man, and who will return when we least expect it.

Nobody saw it coming — least of all me.
     — Cameron Mills on his unexpected career at Kentucky

God continually does the unexpected,
like showing up as Jesus,
who will return unexpectedly.

JUST PERFECT

Read Matthew 5:43-48.

"Be perfect, therefore, as your heavenly Father is perfect"
(v. 48).

The University of Kentucky once had a football team so perfect that it was not only undefeated and untied but unscored on.

They became known as the "Immortals of '98," that bunch from the school known then as Kentucky State College who went 7-0 and outscored their opponents 180-0.

Many athletes were off fighting in the Spanish-American War, and State's schedule for 1897 reflected the unusual times. Among the seven games were the usual suspects such as Centre College, but also Company H of the 8th Massachusetts and a picked team of two divisions of soldiers from Indiana.

The only close game of the season was an illusion. The record shows that State beat Centre 6-0, but the game was called after fifteen minutes of play when a storm washed away both the field and the spectators. "With no one to cheer them on, the two teams decided to call it quits."

Left guard J.W. Graham said the toughest game was with "that bunch of picked soldiers." The Indiana lads bet about $25,000 on the game, not that they would win, but that they would score on the 5-0 State team. They lost the game and the bet 17-0.

Professor A.M. Miller, the "daddy" of UK football (See Devotion No. 86.) protested that Kentucky University (Transylvania) had a couple of ringers. The team played two soldiers who registered at the school, played in the game, and then dropped out — in one day. Miller dropped his protest after State won the game 18-0.

The team's success ultimately laid the foundation for organized football at the school. The faculty committee overseeing athletics had refused a request for funds in 1897, but appropriated $150 annually after the "Immortals'" season.

Nobody's perfect; we all make mistakes every day. We botch our personal relationships; at work we seek competence, not perfection. To insist upon personal or professional perfection in our lives is to establish an impossibly high standard that will eventually destroy us physically, emotionally, and mentally.

Yet that is exactly the standard God sets for us. Our love is to be perfect, never ceasing, never failing, never qualified — just the way God loves us. And Jesus didn't limit his command to only preachers and goody-two-shoes types. All of his disciples are to be perfect as they navigate their way through the world's ambiguous definition and understanding of love.

But that's impossible! Well, not necessarily, if to love perfectly is to serve God wholeheartedly and to follow Jesus with single-minded devotion. Anyhow, in his perfect love for us, God makes allowance for our imperfect love and the consequences of it in the perfection of Jesus.

If we chase perfection, we can catch excellence.

— *Vince Lombardi*

**In his perfect love for us, God provides a way
for us to escape the consequences
of our imperfect love for him: Jesus.**

KENTUCKY

DAY 47

A CHANGE OF PLANS

Read Genesis 18:20-33.

"The Lord said, 'If I find fifty righteous people in the city of Sodom, I will spare the whole place for their sake'" (v. 26).

After he got a phone call that included a death threat, Adolph Rupp changed his mind about a player.

Six days prior to the beginning of the 1956-57 basketball season, Billy Thompson of the *Lexington Herald-Leader* called the UK head coach for an interview. During the course of their conversation, Thompson asked Rupp to name his starting lineup and the coach obliged.

Thompson looked over the names and then told the coach he had not mentioned "a pretty fair country ball player in sophomore Johnny Cox." Cox had been a star on the UK freshman team after leading Hazard High School to the 1955 state title. Rupp replied, "Johnny just hasn't been looking too good in practice." The writer asked the coach if he could use that in a column, and Rupp told him to go ahead.

Later, Rupp told Thompson that the afternoon the column hit the streets, he got a phone call "so hot that he dropped it." A more than slightly irate and partisan fan from Hazard informed Rupp that "if Johnny Cox wasn't in the starting lineup for the opening game, there would be a hanging of a coach in Lexington, and it wouldn't be in effigy."

WILDCATS

Rupp said to Thompson, "You know, that darned boy started looking better that very afternoon."

In fact, Cox looked pretty good all three seasons of his eligibility at UK. A forward, he was first-team All-SEC three times and was third-team All-America as a sophomore that same season the very angry fan prompted the head coach to change his mind. Cox was first-team All-America his senior season of 1958-59. His jersey number 24 was later retired.

To be unable to adapt to changing circumstances to is stultify and die. It's true of animal life, of business and industry, of the military, of sports teams, of you and your relationships, your job, and your finances.

Changing your plans regularly therefore is rather routine for you. But consider how remarkable it is that the God of the universe may change his mind about something. What could bring that about?

Prayer. Someone — a desert-dwelling nomad named Abraham or even a 21st-century Kentucky fan like you — talks to God, who listens and considers what is asked of him.

You may feel uncomfortable praying. Maybe you're reluctant and embarrassed; perhaps you feel you're not very good at it. But nobody majors in prayer at school, and as for being reluctant, what have you got to lose? Your answer may even be a change of plans on God's part. Such is the power of prayer.

I've changed my mind about it: Instead of being bad, it stinks.
— Baseball Hall-of-Famer Sparky Anderson on the designated hitter

Prayer is powerful;
it may even change God's mind.

DAY 48

ONE-MAN ARMY

Read Revelation 19:11-21.

*"The rest of them were killed by the sword that came out
of the mouth of the rider on the horse" (v. 21).*

Just ask Tennessee: Lou Michaels was perfectly capable of being a one-man army on the football field.

Michaels played tackle for the Cats from 1955-57 and was All-America the last two seasons. He was the SEC's Most Valuable Player in '57 and was fourth in the voting for the Heisman Trophy. UK retired his jersey number (79) in 1990; he was inducted into the College Football Hall of Fame in 1992.

Michaels provided a great example of his versatility in the 1956 game against Georgia Tech. He stopped the Tech runner cold on fourth down inside the UK one; on the next play, he boomed a 61-yard punt that moved Tech back to its 39.

"Football was my game," Michaels said. "I loved it. I wanted to eat, sleep, and live it." Teammate Billy Mitchell, a halfback who later was a UK assistant coach, said of Michaels, "He was the only guy I ever knew who loved to practice."

Michaels was so indispensable to the Wildcats that he played all but 44 minutes of the 1957 season. He was the main reason the Cats pulled off a stunning 20-6 upset of the Vols that year. He got UK off and running by recovering a fumble in the end zone for his only collegiate touchdown. He then kicked the extra point.

Only a few seconds later, Michaels blasted a punt into the UT end zone and made the tackle on the return, forcing a fumble that Jim Urbaniak recovered. That set up a four-yard touchdown run by Bob Cravens. Again, Michaels kicked the PAT.

He dominated Tennessee on defense, benefitting from a move to middle linebacker for the first time. The coaches' only instructions to him were "Where the football is, you go get it." He did just that, as the Vols couldn't run away from him. He was in effect a one-man army in a huge Kentucky win.

A similar situation will occur when Christ returns. He will not come back to us as the meek lamb who was led unprotestingly to slaughter on the cross. Instead, he will be a one-man army, a rider on a white horse who will destroy those forces responsible for disorder and chaos in God's world.

This image of our Jesus as a warrior may well shock and discomfort us; it should also excite and thrill us. It reminds us vividly that God will unleash his awesome power to effect justice and righteousness in a world that persecutes his people and slanders his name. It should also lend us a sense of urgency because the time will pass when decisions for Christ can still be made.

For now, Jesus has an army at his disposal in the billions of Christians around the world. We are Christian soldiers; we have a world to conquer for our Lord — before he returns as a one-man army to finish the job.

On the day we played Tennessee, [Lou Michaels] was the greatest player in America.
  — UK line coach Clarence 'Buckshot' Underwood on the '57 UT game

Jesus will return as a one-man army to conquer the forces of evil; for now, we are his army.

DAY 49

CHEAP TRICKS

Read Acts 19:11-20.

"The evil spirit answered them, 'Jesus I know, and I know about Paul, but who are you?'" (v. 15)

Players who tried to pull tricks on Joe B. Hall and his coaches found out that fake blood didn't work but a tiny girlfriend did.

Ronnie Lyons played on Adolph Rupp's last team and for Hall from (1971-74). He was second-team All-SEC as a sophomore and was named the Outstanding Senior in '74.

It was well known that Lyons was a big fan of wrestling. One year during the Christmas holidays when the other students had gone home, Hall hired a retired gentleman to handle security for his players in Holmes Hall. He awoke the coach one night and in a panic-stricken voice told Hall to hurry over. "The boys got to wrasslin," he said, "and I think they've killed Jim Duff," who was a walk-on player. "He's covered with blood and I'm not sure if he's still breathing or not," the excited security guard said.

Hall didn't buy it. He ordered the guard to go back into the room "and tell Jim Duff to get up, wipe all the ketchup off and get to the phone." He then added, "Tell him to bring Ronnie Lyons with him because I know whose idea this wrestling match was."

Decades later, Lyons still marveled at how Hall was able to see through every trick he came up with.

The coaches missed one, though, thanks to a petite girlfriend. A player who lived in Wildcat Lodge received a surprise visit one night from his "pretty and petite girlfriend," and she was still in the room when the one o'clock curfew passed.

The other players figured the worst when they saw the coaches pulling bed check: They would all be running wind sprints at five in the morning. To their surprise though, a coach checked the room and left without saying anything.

The befuddled players rushed into the room seeking an explanation. The player pulled out one of the large drawers in his dresser to reveal that tiny little girlfriend crammed inside.

We all have to be wary of tricks being pulled by scam artists these days. An e-mail encourages you to send money to a foreign country to get rich. That guy at your front door offers to resurface your driveway at a ridiculously low price. A TV ad promises a pill to help you lose weight without diet or exercise.

You've been around; you check things out before deciding. The same approach is necessary with spiritual matters, too, because false religions and bogus Christian denominations abound. The key is what any group does with Jesus. Is he the son of God, the ruler of the universe, and the only way to salvation? If not, then the group espouses something other than the true Word of God.

The good news about Jesus does indeed sound too good to be true. But the only catch is that there is no catch. No trick — just the truth.

When you run trick plays and they work, you're a genius. But when they don't work, folks question your sanity.

— *Bobby Bowden*

God's promises through Jesus sound too good to be true, but the only catch is that there is no catch.

THE RIGHT MAN

Interesting!!!

Read Exodus 3:1-12.

"So now, go. I am sending you to Pharaoh to bring my people the Israelites out of Egypt" (v. 10).

One of the new coach's players was instrumental in making sure Kentucky got the right man for the job.

John Mauer coached the UK basketball team to a 40-16 record over three seasons. After the 1929-30 season, he quit because the school refused to give him a pay raise.

Among those considered to replace Mauer was Adolph Rupp, who had made a name for himself with a four-year record of 59-21 at a high school near Chicago. Though he was thinking of giving up coaching for a job with better pay, the 29-year-old coach decided to see what UK had to offer.

Two university officials met him at the train station on a spring day in 1930. They saw "a strong young man standing about 6-foot-2, a little on the portly side." He was "dressed conservatively, combed his hair neatly, spit-shined his shoes, and carried himself well." One person said Rupp looked like a preacher.

They rode through Lexington past a slum and arrived late for lunch, dining on cold fish, corn bread, and coffee. Rupp's first impression was that "the people of Kentucky had poor houses, and they also didn't eat so good."

Among the athletic council members who interviewed Rupp was freshman Ellis Johnson. He was the student representative, but he was also on the basketball team. He would have a voice in hiring his own coach. As it turned out, he had a key voice and lobbied actively for Rupp's hiring.

The council agreed. History proved, or course, that Rupp was the right man for the job as he went on to win more games than any other coach in college basketball history at the time. Johnson was a three-year starter and was All-America as a senior.

What do you want to be when you grow up? Somehow you are supposed to know the answer to that question when you're a teenager, the time in life when common sense and logic are at their lowest ebb. Long after those halcyon teen years are left behind, you may make frequent career changes. You chase the job that gives you not just financial rewards but also some personal satisfaction and sense of accomplishment.

God, too, wants you in the right job, one that he has designed specifically for you. Though Moses protested that he wasn't the right man, he was indeed God's anointed one, the right man to do exactly what God needed done.

There's a little Moses in all of us. Like him, we shrink before the tasks God calls us to. Like him also, we have God-given abilities, talents, and passions. The right man or women for any job is the one who works and achieves not for self but for the glory of God.

Because he told us he was the best basketball coach in the United States and convinced us he was.
— Athletic council member when asked why they hired Adolph Rupp

Working for God's glory and not your own
makes you the right person for the job,
no matter what it may be.

PAIN RELIEF

Read 2 Corinthians 1:3-7.

"Just as the sufferings of Christ flow over into our lives, so also through Christ our comfort overflows" (v. 5).

Dicky Beal would never recommend Coach Joe B. Hall's training-table regimen to anyone else, but it was effective.

Beal was "a 5'10" dynamo" of a guard who played from 1980-84 and "captured the hearts of the fans." His senior season was a 29-win campaign that netted an SEC championship and a trip to the NCAA championship game.

Early in the season, though, Beal's effectiveness was limited by his failure to recover completely from multiple knee surgeries. He limped badly early on and later confessed, "I was never 100 percent that year, but with all the talent on that team, I didn't feel I had to be completely healthy." He said the team needed someone to spread the ball around and play defense, "and I could still do all those things."

But he wasn't doing them as well as he could if he were healthy, and Hall saw it. "He knew I was having trouble getting full range of motion with my knee," Beal recalled.

So Hall called the surgeon who had operated on Beal's knee and asked him if some residual scar tissue, which should have already have been broken down, were slowing Beal down. That Beal still favored the knee indicated the tissue was a real possibility, the doctor replied.

WILDCATS

Then Hall had a rather gruesome question. He asked the doctor if he would do any further damage to Beal's knee if he grabbed him by the ankle and snapped it against his thigh to break up the tissue. The doctor said it was worth a try.

So without giving Beal any warning — since the senior might well have understandably refused — Hall found him on the training table, walked up to him, told him to relax, and pulled the lower leg "through a full range of motion." As Hall recalled it, "Dicky let out a blood-curdling scream and looked at me like I was crazy, but from that day on, he started moving better."

Since you live on Earth and not in Heaven, you are forced to play with pain as Dicky Beal did. Whether it's a car wreck that left you shattered, the end of a relationship that left you battered, or a loved one's death that left you tattered — pain finds you and challenges you to keep going.

While God's word teaches that you will reap what you sow, life also teaches that pain and hardship are not necessarily the result of personal failure. Pain in fact can be one of the tools God uses to mold your character and change your life.

What are you to do when you are hit full-speed by the awful pain that seems to choke the very will to live out of you? Where is your consolation, your comfort, and your help?

In almighty God, whose love will never fail. When life knocks you to your knees, you're closer to God than ever before.

It hurts up to a point and then it doesn't get any worse.
> — *Ultramarathon runner Ann Trason*

**When life hits you with pain, you can always
turn to God for comfort, consolation, and hope.**

WORRYWART

Read Matthew 6:25-34.

"Therefore I tell you, do not worry about your life, what you will eat or drink; or about your body, what you will wear" (v. 25a).

Kentucky head football coach Harry Gamage was such a consistent worrier that he earned the nickname "Gloomy Harry."

Gamage, who coached in Lexington from 1927-33, "was one of those natural worriers who always entered a season or a game as if a little black cloud hung over his head." Perhaps Gamage had some reason behind his gloomy outlook as he arrived from Illinois to make UK one of the leading teams in the South.

For one thing, the university didn't offer athletic scholarships per se. Joe Rupert, an end and the team captain in 1934, recalled that his scholarship consisted of tuition and a job with a downtown business. "We worked two or three hours in the evenings to earn $7 per week, which was ample in those days to pay for three large meals per day and a clean bed to sleep in," he said.

Gamage was described as "debonair" with movie-star looks. His pessimistic outlook was so well known that *The Atlanta Journal* ran a piece in the fall of 1932 that described Gamage meeting up with the author, the "Old Timer." The latter said to the coach, "I assume you are beset with injuries, poor material, hookworm and malaria among your squad: your quarterbacks are morons in intellect, your linemen are victims of malnutrition, and the

WILDCATS

depression has just reached your fair city." Gamage replied, "Mr. Timer, your imagination is inadequate and fails utterly to portray the actual dire situation."

Despite his propensity for pessimism and worrying, Gamage was the most successful football coach UK had seen so far. He stayed on the job for seven seasons, the longest stint of a Kentucky coach to that time. He also won 32 games, at that point the most of any Wildcat football coach in school history.

"Don't worry, be happy," Jesus admonishes, which is easy for him to say. He never had a mortgage payment to meet or had teenagers in the house. He was in perfect health, never had marital problems, and knew exactly what he wanted to do with his life.

The truth is we do worry. And in the process we lose sleep, the joy in our lives, and even our faith. To worry is to place ourselves in danger of destroying our health, our relationships with those we love, and even our relationship with God. No wonder Jesus said not to worry.

Being Jesus, he doesn't just offer us a sound bite; he gives us instructions for a worry-free life. We must serve God and not the gods of the world, we must trust God and not ourselves, and we must seek God's kingdom and his righteousness.

In other words, when we use our lives to take care of God's business, God uses his love and his power to take care of ours.

If you don't like to worry, why do it? It won't help your performance.
— Joe Namath

Worrying is a clear sign we are about our own business rather than God's.

DAY 53

IMPOSSIBLE DREAM

Read Matthew 19:16-26.

"Jesus looked at them and said, 'With man this is impossible, but with God all things are possible'" (v. 26).

It was "an impossible dream come true," said one writer.

The nation's all-time winningest basketball program and the second all-time winner met on Jan. 3, 2004. As usual, the court was littered with all-stars, prize recruits, and future pro players. That would be, of course, Kentucky vs. North Carolina.

So when the final horn sounded and the Cats had a thrilling 61-56 win, the hero of the night — the guy who got a standing ovation when he walked over for the Player of the Game radio interview — was a walk-on whose most fervent recruiters out of high school had been Transylvania and Centre. That would be somewhat bedazzled sophomore guard Ravi Moss, the guy hugging the game ball to his chest and soaking in the wildly enthusiastic applause from more than 23,000 fans in Rupp Arena.

Moss, of course, didn't carry the Cats to the big win all by himself. Guard Gerald Fitch scored 21 points and hit the shot of the game, a three-pointer with 24 seconds left. Forward Erik Daniels dropped in 18 points and pulled down 10 rebounds.

But nothing about the game brought more delight to head Cat Tubby Smith and the Rupp denizens than Moss' play. He had four points, three rebounds, and one assist, and played some sterling defense in ten "unforeseen but unafraid minutes."

Moss came to UK with an academic scholarship and an invitation to walk on. He wasn't even a bit player until Smith suddenly barked out his name with 13 minutes to play. "I WAS somewhat surprised," Moss admitted. He was in the game at the end, relentlessly guarding a Tar Heel who surely had never heard of him.

On his way out of Rupp, "Moss got the full star treatment: autographs, back slaps, and a bear hug" from the coach's wife. "A dream come true," admitted Moss, who shot driveway hoops growing up while impossibly envisioning himself wearing UK blue.

Let's face it. Any pragmatic person, no matter how deep his faith, has to admit that we have succeeded in turning God's beautiful world into an impossible mess. The only hope for this dying, sin-infested place lies in our Lord's return to set everything right.

But we can't just give up and sit around praying for Jesus' return, as glorious a day as that will be. Our mission in this world is to change it for Jesus. We serve a Lord who calls us to step out in faith into seemingly impossible situations. We serve a Lord so audacious that he inspires us to believe that we are the instruments through which God does the impossible.

Changing the world may indeed seem impossible, but so did what Ravi Moss accomplished against UNC. Changing our corner of the world is not impossible at all. It is, rather, a very possible, doable act of faith and commitment.

The difference between the impossible and the possible lies in a person's determination.
— *Former major league manager Tommy Lasorda*

**With God, nothing is impossible,
including changing the world for Jesus.**

GOD'S WRATH

Read Romans 2:1-11.

"Because of your stubbornness and your unrepentant heart, you are storing up wrath against yourself for the day of God's wrath, when his righteous judgment will be revealed" (v.5).

As Allen Feldhaus learned, even a Wildcat who hadn't been in the game was safe from the wrath of Adolph Rupp.

Feldhaus was a 6-5 forward who played for the basketball Cats from 1959-62 and also lettered in baseball. His son, Deron, played for Kentucky from 1988-92 and had his jersey number 12 retired.

Allen had to battle for playing time though he appeared in or started 72 games in his three seasons of eligibility. In the first half of the Auburn game of his junior year, he didn't play at all. If a game wasn't going too well, the players would scramble to avoid being the first one on the bench in the dressing room at halftime so as to increase the likelihood of escaping Rupp's wrath. On this night, the game wasn't going well at all, and the head Cat was angry and upset with his team's performance.

As Feldhaus remembered it, Rupp would "start yelling and go right down the line and just chew on everybody." Since he hadn't played any, Feldhaus had beaten the rush to the dressing room and had maneuvered into a seat way in the back. "I thought, 'Well, he is not going to get on me tonight. I haven't been in the game.'"

He was wrong. Rupp moved right on down the bench, chewing

on each player in his turn. He didn't even slow down when he got to Feldhaus, lighting right into him with his usual vehemence. Assistant coach Harry Lancaster interrupted the fussing coach to point out, "Coach, Feldhaus hasn't been in the game."

Rupp didn't even hesitate. "I don't care," he said. "He still hasn't done anything to help us."

God is love, mercy, and grace; that aspect of God we embrace. The Bible is very clear, however, that God's character also includes justice, wrath, and judgment. We don't like that part. So to escape accountability and responsibility in and for our lives, we declare with our spiritual fingers crossed that a God of love could never condemn anyone to Hell.

In reality, the wrath of God is another example of his abiding love for us. Judgment Day is in effect a sorting day, sort of like a divine bunk assignment at summer camp. God dispenses to those who deny Jesus and God in their lives exactly what they have said they desired: eternity without God. Those who have lived their lives in service to Christ get what they desire: eternity with God.

God doesn't condemn anyone to Hell because he doesn't make that decision. Rather, we make it by the way we live. God just provides the means for each of us to get to where we've said we always wanted to go, be it Heaven or Hell.

Maybe if you put me in, I could help you.
        — Allen Feldhaus' thoughts after Rupp chewed him out

**God's wrath ultimately reveals itself in sacrificial
love, giving those who have denied him
what they wish for: eternity without him.**

DAY 55

THE GOOD FIGHT

Read 1 Corinthians 10:1-6.

"Though we live in the world, we do not wage war as the world does. The weapons we fight with are not the weapons of the world" (vv. 3-4a).

We're in a street fight. I'm in a street fight. I want to see who has my back." As it turned out, all eighty Wildcat football players had head coach Joker Phillips's back.

With his team trailing 10th-ranked South Carolina 28-10 at halftime on Oct. 16, 2010, the Kentucky head football coach told his team "it was time for them to put up their dukes" and come out fighting the last half. They did just that, throwing one haymaker after another at the dazed Gamecocks. The defense shut out South Carolina in the last half while the offense scored 21 unanswered points for a stirring and stunning 31-28 win.

"All our defense did is come out in the second half and give up 103 yards and throw a shutout to one of the best offenses in the conference," an elated Phillips said after the game.

"We never lost faith," said Kentucky's do-it-all star, Randall Cobb about the way the team kept fighting even though the Cats were way behind one of the best teams in the country. "We never for one second thought we were going to lose that game."

There were probably quite a few doubters among the UK faithful at halftime. But the Cats fought their way to within 28-23 and then got the ball at their own 32 with 7:31 left. Quarterback Mike

WILDCATS

Hartline led the team to a fourth-and seven at the USC 24 where he lofted a strike to Cobb for the game winner with 1:15 to play. Cobb then fought his way in for the two-point conversion.

The Gamecocks raced to the UK 20 with 11 seconds left. Head Gamecock Steve Spurrier opted to go for the win, but the Cats still had some fight left. Reserve cornerback Cartier Rice tipped the end-zone pass into the open arms of defensive back Anthony Mosley for the game-clinching interception.

Violence is not the Christian way, but what about confrontation? Following Jesus' admonition to turn the other cheek has rendered many a Christian meek and mild in the name of obedience. But we need to remember that the Lord we follow once bullwhipped a bunch of folks who turned God's temple into a flea market.

With Christianity in America under attack as never before, we must stand up for and fight for our faith. Who else is there to stand up for Jesus if not you? Our pretty little planet — including our nation — is a battleground between good and evil. We are far from helpless in this fight because God has provided us with a powerful set of weapons. Prayer, faith, hope, love, the Word of God itself and the Holy Spirit — these are the weapons at our command with which to vanquish evil and godlessness.

We are called by God to use them, to fight the good fight, not just in our own lives but in our nation and in our world.

We came with 80 guys, and all 80 of them had my back.
— *Joker Phillips*

**'Stand Up, Stand Up for Jesus' is not
an antiquated hymn but is a contemporary
call to battle for our Lord.**

DAY 56

THE SUB

Read Galatians 3:10-14.

"Christ redeemed us from the curse of the law by becoming a curse for us" (v. 13).

Substitutes are known to bail teams out quite frequently. But the sub of a sub?

Marquis Estill was the third-string center on the 2000-2001 UK team behind starter Jason Parker and backup Marvin Stone. He failed to score a point or grab a rebound in the Cats' 72-68 defeat of Holy Cross in the opening round of the NCAA Tournament.

Thus, Estill didn't figure to be much of a factor in the second-round game against Iowa. In fact, he was so ignored by the media during the interview session prior to the Iowa game that he apparently fell asleep. "I wasn't asleep," he said. "I was just laid back and trying to relax."

Despite Estill's expectations of seeing little action against the Hawkeyes, he nevertheless worked himself up for the game by watching *Remember the Titans* later that night. "I felt good and had a lot of energy," he said.

He needed it. The sub of a sub was the difference in the game. That's according to the Iowa head coach.

Early on, Iowa's center "looked like he could chew up and spit out UK's post players." He got Parker out of the game with two fouls at 16:45 of the first half. Stone didn't contribute much over the next five minutes. In what seemed like a move born of desperation, Estill went into the game with 11:53 left in the half. He not only shut down the Iowa big man the rest of the half, he scored 11 points and grabbed five rebounds.

The Cats broke a 33-33 tie by scoring the last twelve points of the half. They were never headed after that, winning 92-79.

And the sub's sub? He scored a career-high 22 points on 9-of-11 shooting, nabbed six boards, and shut down the Iowa center most of the game. "The rims are nice out there," Estill said about his scoring spree.

Wouldn't it be cool if you had a substitute like Marquis Estill for life's hard stuff? Have to tell everyone of a death in the family? Call in your sub. Breaking up with your boyfriend? Job interview? Chemistry test? Big presentation at work? Let the sub handle it.

We do have such a substitute, but not for the matters of life. Instead, Jesus is our substitute for matters of life and death. Since Jesus has already made it, we don't have to make the sacrifice God demands for forgiveness and salvation.

One of the ironies of our age is that many people desperately grope for a substitute for Jesus. Mysticism, human philosophies such as Scientology, false religions such as Hinduism and Islam, cults, New Age approaches that preach self-fulfillment without responsibility or accountability — they and others like them are all pitiful, inadequate substitutes for Jesus.

Accept no substitutes. It's Jesus or nothing.

They probably didn't know too much about me. A lot of teams don't.
— *Substitute Marquis Estill on the Iowa game*

There is no substitute for Jesus,
the consummate substitute.

DAY 57

SIZE MATTERS

Read Luke 19:1-10.

*[Zacchaeus] wanted to see who Jesus was, but being a
short man he could not, because of the crowd. So he ran
ahead and climbed a sycamore-fig tree to see him (vv. 3-4).*

They were a bunch of runts whom nobody expected anything
of. So much for size.

Adolph Rupp's team of 1965-66 was so small it became part of
Wildcat lore as "Rupp's Runts." The tallest starter was Tom Kron,
who may have been 6-foot-6. Pat Riley was a 6-foot-3 forward
who jumped center. Rupp taught him to get up first, jump off both
legs, and dig an elbow into the other guy's shoulder for leverage.
By riding the opponent's shoulder, Riley lost only twelve of fifty-
eight jumps and once beat a seven-footer to the ball.

The Cats were coming off a lackluster 15-10 season and had lost
three seniors: Randy Embry, Terry Mobley, and John Adams. Com-
bine that with the obvious lack of height, and the team was one
"that people didn't have a whole lot of faith in," Riley said. "We
were very small, . . . so we started out in the preseason as a team
that wouldn't be one of the contenders."

The Runts had to do something to compensate for their lack of
size. They did. As longtime Rupp assistant coach Harry Lancaster
put it, the Runts were "one of the finest we ever had for moving
the basketball. . . . They were so intelligent and even though small
they were very quick."

WILDCATS

That lack of size was evident the first time what would be the starting five took the floor: They averaged 6-foot-3. But they used that quickness and that on-court intelligence and team chemistry to transform themselves into one of the greatest teams in Wildcat basketball history. Rupp would "close his eyes and listen to the pit-pat of the ball being passed to perfection."

The Runts won twenty-three straight before they lost and went all the way to the championship game of the NCAA Tournament. They finished the season with an incredible 32-2 record.

Bigger is better! Such is one of the most powerful mantras of our time. We expand our basketball arenas. We augment our body parts. Hey, make that a triple cheeseburger and a large order of fries! My company is bigger than your company. Even our church buildings must be bigger to be better. About the only exception to our all-consuming drive for bigness is our waistlines.

But size obviously didn't matter to Jesus. After all, salvation came to the house of an evil tax collector who was so short he had to climb a tree to catch a glimpse of Jesus. Zacchaeus indeed had a big bank account; he was a big man in town even if his own people scorned him. But none of that — including Zacchaeus' height — mattered; Zacchaeus received salvation because of his repentance, which revealed itself in a changed life.

The same is true for us today. What matters is the size of the heart devoted to our Lord.

It is not the size of a man but the size of his heart that matters.
— Evander Holyfield

Size matters to Jesus, but only the size of the heart of the one who would follow Him.

WORK ETHIC

Read Matthew 9:35-38.

"Then he said to his disciples, 'The harvest is plentiful but the workers are few. Ask the Lord of the harvest, therefore, to send out workers into his harvest field'" (vv. 37-38).

For a boy named Adolph Rupp, life was "dawn-to-dusk toil in the fields, and a close family relationship that resulted from the battle for survival on the prairie."

A solid grounding in the work ethic was part of Rupp's childhood that shaped him as a man and a coach and helped make him a legend. He grew up in central Kansas, one of six children of German Mennonite immigrants. Life on the farm was hard, and the work got harder when his father died when Adolph was 9.

While the older boys worked the fields, young Adolph milked the cows, fed the hogs, and performed other light chores as his hard-working mother assigned. When he was 10, he took his turn on the mowing machine, which kept him in the fields all day long.

When he was 13, Adolph joined a threshing-machine crew. He ate breakfast by the light of a kerosene lamp and was in the field when the sun showed up. He helped farm various crops even after he graduated from high school and once said he most dreaded the monotonous job of plowing the half-mile-long Kansas corn rows. His favorite time was haymaking, when the neighbors gathered "for hard work, clean fun, and plenty of gossip."

As he grew older, Adolph joined his brothers in breaking wild horses for some extra money. He worked as the school janitor, the first to arrive in the morning to get the fires started to heat the building. "He swept the floor, wiped blackboards, dusted erasers, and filled coal buckets, all for fifty cents a month."

So they could go to school during the harsh winters, the Rupp boys rented a house in town. Adolph worked odd jobs, mostly at a local grocery store, to pay expenses. In the summer, he kept up his work with the threshing crew, working all day, bathing in a creek, and sleeping outdoors on straw.

Adolph Rupp knew all about hard work.

Do you embrace hard work or try to avoid it? No matter how hard you may try, you really can't escape hard work. Funny thing about all these labor-saving devices like cell phones and laptop computers: You're working longer and harder than ever. For many of us, our work defines us perhaps more than any other aspect of our lives. But there's a workforce you're a part of that doesn't show up in any Labor Department statistics or any IRS records.

You're part of God's staff; God has a specific job that only you can do for him. It's often referred to as a "calling," but it amounts to your serving God where there is a need in the way that best suits your God-given abilities and talents.

You should stand ready to work for God all the time, 24-7. Those are awful hours, but the benefits are out of this world.

It was hard work from sunup until sundown. I enjoyed that.
— Adolph Rupp on his work threshing grain

God calls you to work for him using the talents
and gifts he gave you; whether you're a worker
or a malingerer is up to you.

STILL THE SAME

Read Hebrews 13:5-16.

"Jesus Christ is the same yesterday and today and forever" (v. 8).

An exploding football. A player who was an engineer with the City of Lexington. Arbitrary time limits for games. This was the wild, wacky, and woolly world of UK football in its early days.

Kentucky State (later UK) halfback Jake Gaiser, who lettered from 1909-11, recalled that a big pile-up during a scrimmage left the ball carrier feeling around for the ball. What he found wasn't usable. It had exploded during the mad scramble.

J. White Guyn, who coached the team from 1906-08, actually earned a fifth varsity letter in football in 1905 after he graduated and while he was working as an engineer for the City of Lexington. He recalled that he strolled into Stoll Field on the afternoon of a football game and his former teammates pressed him into service. As Guyn recalled it, "While they huddled around me, I hastily donned a substitute's jersey and played the second half. Sure, the other team griped but nothing came of it."

For several years, the time limits for games were set by the teams before the kickoff. This allowed head coach E.R. Sweetland (1909-10, 1912) to snooker Illinois in 1909 and pull off "Kentucky's most important victory up to that time." Somehow, he got into the contract the stipulation that the game would consist of 15-minute halves. When Illinois officials asked for a longer game, Sweetland

WILDCATS

delivered a classic sob story. He told them that his players were so small and so affected by the heat that they just couldn't play any longer than that. However, he "would consider going on with the game if the men were able to stand it."

Richard Barbee scored early on an overconfident Illinois team, and State was about to score again when the 30 minutes were up. Illinois didn't ask for an extension and took a 6-2 loss.

Like everything else, football has changed since those early days. Laptops and smart phones, high definition TVs and IMAX theaters — they and much that is common in your life now may not have even been around when you were 16. Think about how style, cars, communications, and tax laws constantly change.

You shouldn't be too harsh on this old world, though, because you've changed also. You've aged, gained or lost weight, gotten married, changed jobs, or relocated.

Change in our contemporary times is often so rapid that it is bewildering and confusing, leaving us casting about for something to hold on to that will always be the same, that we can use as an anchor for our lives. Is there anything in this world like that; is there anything that is impervious to change?

Sadly, the answer's no. All the things of this world change.

On the other hand, there's Jesus, who is the same today and the same forever, always dependable, always loving you. No matter what happens in our lives, Jesus is still the same.

I'm not too proud to change. I like to win too much.
— Bobby Bowden

**Jesus is the same forever;
his love for you will never change.**

DAY 60

MIRACLE PLAY

Read Matthew 12:38-42.

*"He answered, 'A wicked and adulterous generation asks
for a miraculous sign!'" (v. 39)*

Down by six with 31 seconds to play against the fifth-ranked
team in the country in the era before the three-point shot. It would
take a miracle to win — but the Wildcats did it.

On Dec. 9, 1978, Kansas led the Cats 66-60 with those 31 seconds
left in overtime. Freshman guard Dwight Anderson scored four
points on a layup and two free throws, but that left the Jayhawks
with a two-point lead and the ball with only 10 seconds to play.

Anderson struck again, getting his hands on the inbounds pass
and then sailing it across the court where Kyle Macy grabbed it.
He nailed a 15-foot jumper that tied the game as the stunned
crowd at Rupp Arena couldn't quite believe what it had just seen.

But the miraculous comeback had netted only a tie, and only one
more miracle could avoid overtime and a possible Jayhawk win.
But a miracle — or a miscue — did happen.

A Kansas player signalled for a time out — but the Hawks had
used them all. Technical foul. Macy, who still holds the school
career record for free-throw percentage (89%) went to the line
with a miraculous chance to win the game that had seemed so
out of reach only a few seconds before.

Macy never varied his unusual routine at the line. "I would
line up my toe right in the middle of the free-throw stripe," he

described. "Then I would dry my fingers by reaching down and grabbing both socks." But there was more. "Then it was dribble three times, take a deep breath, bend at the knees a little more than most free-throw shooters, sight the basket and let it go."

One again, Macy was true, and the Rupp-Arena crowd had just witnessed a miraculous comeback that would make this game a part of Wildcat legend and lore.

Miracles defy rational explanation. Like coming from six points down in 31 seconds to win. Escaping with minor abrasions from an accident that totals your car. Recovering from an illness that seemed terminal.

Underlying the notion of miracles is the idea that they are rare instances of direct divine intervention that reveal glimpses of God to us. But life shows us quite the contrary, that miracles are anything but rare. Since God created the world and everything in it, everything around you is miraculous. Even you are a miracle.

Your life thus can be mundane, dull, and ordinary, or it can be spent in a glorious attitude of childlike wonder and awe. It all depends on whether or not you see the world through the eyes of faith. Only through faith can you discern the hand of God in any event; only through faith can you see the miraculous and thus see God.

Jesus knew that miracles don't produce faith, but rather faith produces miracles.

I had to use some body English and almost walk it in.
   — Kyle Macy on his free throw that completed a Wildcat miracle

**Miracles are all around us,
but it takes the eyes of faith to see them.**

PAYBACK

Read Matthew 5:38-42.

"I tell you, Do not resist an evil person. If someone strikes you on the right cheek, turn to him the other also" (v. 39).

Scott Padgett got his revenge, but he lost the ball.

Padgett grew up a Kentucky fan and watched the Kentucky-Duke classic in the 1992 NCAA Tournament in horror. "I couldn't believe it," he recalled. "I was just in shock."

Six years later, in 1998, Padgett was a junior forward for the Wildcats with a chance to exact some revenge on Duke when the two met in the NCAA regional finals. "For Kentucky kids who saw Duke beat Kentucky in 1992, [the game] did mean more to us," Padgett said.

In what became known as "The Revenge Game," the Cats battled back from a 17-point deficit and took the lead before Duke tied the game at 81 with about 30 seconds left. Padgett set a screen for star point guard Wayne Turner, who had been killing Duke all day. The defense moved over to Turner, leaving Padgett for a wide-open three. Turner got the ball to him, and he hit it. Unable to contain his excitement, Padgett ran down the court yelling and screaming, "We got this!"

Not yet, though. As the clock wound down, Duke trailed 86-84 and had the ball and 4.5 seconds to play. The Blue Devils had needed only 2.1 seconds in 1992 to snatch victory from certain defeat. Not this time. Coach Tubby Smith elected to guard the inbounds man, and with no time outs, Duke could manage only a wild half-court shot that fell harmlessly into Padgett's arms.

Padgett and his Wildcats had their revenge, but Padgett still regrets what happened next. "I should own that [game] ball right now," he said years later. In his excitement, though, he "threw it up in the air. To this day, I wish I still had that ball." Instead captain Jeff Sheppard, who had 18 points and 11 rebounds, grabbed it.

The very nature of an intense rivalry such as Kentucky-Duke is that the loser will seek payback for the defeat of the season before. But what about in life when somebody's done you wrong; is it time to get even?

The problem with revenge in real-life is that it isn't as clear-cut as a scoreboard. Life is so messy that any attempt at revenge is often inadequate or, worse, backfires and injures you.

As a result, you remain gripped by resentment and anger, which hurts you and no one else. You poison your own happiness while that other person goes blithely about her business. The only way someone who has hurt you can keep hurting you is if you're a willing participant.

But it doesn't have to be that way. Jesus ushered in a new way of living when he taught that we are not to seek revenge for personal wrongs and injuries. Let it go and go on with your life. What a relief!

It was a victory that provided payback.
— The New York Times *on the '98 win over Duke*

Resentment and anger over a wrong injures you, not the other person, so forget it — just as Jesus taught.

PRAYER WARRIORS

Read Luke 18:1-8a.

"Then Jesus told his disciples a parable to show them that they should always pray and not give up" (v. 1).

Joe "Red" Hagan's prayer was answered — and Kentucky had a miraculous win.

Hagan lettered as a forward for the Wildcats from 1935-38, playing in every game over those three seasons. He was Second-Team All-SEC and made the league's All-Tournament Team his senior season.

On Feb. 14, 1938, the 9-4 Cats hosted Marquette. Many experts considered the Warriors to be the country's best team, so UK was a big underdog, which seemed to bring the fans out in droves. Every ticket was sold, and "some fans climbed into the rafters, some onto the window sills." They got their money's worth.

The Wildcats took an early 10-point lead, but the relentless Milwaukee boys fought back to tie the game in the closing seconds. As the Cats prepared to inbound the ball, Hagan knelt in the middle of the floor, blessed himself, mumbled a prayer, and then blessed himself again. He got the ball and promptly fired a shot that may well have given head coach Adolph Rupp apoplexy.

But he put the shot up in answer to a direct command. "A voice said to me," Hagan explained after the game, "'Shoot, Hagan, and it will go through the net.'" So he shot it — from near midcourt with 15 seconds on the clock. "Fired with a prayer," the ball caromed off the backboard right through the net. The miraculous shot gave UK a 35-33 lead, and the score stood up when the Warriors couldn't connect on a series of desperate shots.

Exuberant fans stormed onto the floor and carried Hagan on their shoulders into the locker room. In a move that would probably not be countenanced today, Gov. A.B. Chandler got hold of a hammer and a nail and drove the nail into the floor at the spot from which Hagan had launched his prayer-guided shot.

Red Hagan prayed and didn't give up, which is exactly what Jesus taught his followers to do: always pray and never give up.

Any problems we may have with prayer and its results derive from our side, not God's. We pray for a while about something — perhaps fervently at first — but our enthusiasm wanes if we don't receive the answer we want exactly when we want it. Why waste our time by asking for the same thing over and over again?

But God isn't deaf, God does hear our prayers, and God does respond to them. As Jesus clearly taught, our prayers have an impact because they turn the power of Almighty God loose in this world. Thus, falling to our knees and praying to God is not a sign of weakness and helplessness. Rather, praying for someone or something is an aggressive act, an intentional ministry, a conscious attempt on our part to change someone's life or the world for the better.

God responds to our prayers; we often can't perceive or don't understand how he is working to make those prayers come about.

I shot and it went through.
— *Red Hagan, explaining the answer to a prayer*

Jesus taught us to always pray and never give up.

GOOD IDEA

Read Luke 8:40-56.

"In the presence of all the people, she told why she had touched him" (v. 47).

John Calipari had an idea so good that "a team that had been left for dead . . . rallied to fall six points shy of the national title."

By Kentucky's elite standards, Calipari's 2013-14 team with its roster of freshman and sophomore all-stars struggled through the regular season. They started out ranked No. 1 but fell out of the top 25 altogether after dropping the last game of the regular season to Florida. In the SEC, they finished 12-6, tied for a distant second behind the Gators' 18-0 record.

Calipari looked the situation over and had an idea, a "tweak" as it became known. Right before the SEC Tournament, he made the game simpler for freshman point guard Andrew Harrison. He told him to worry less about scoring and more about distributing the ball.

At the first practice after getting his idea, Calipari told Harrison that he would not take a single shot during the scrimmage. "You will create shots. We will chart. We're not telling the team," the head coach said. The results were downright astounding: Harrison had twenty-six assists.

Calipari was furious at himself. "I'm mad the whole practice because it's changed my team. Why didn't I do it earlier?" he fulminated. Then he apologized to Harrison and the team.

WILDCATS

Whether the effects of the infamous "tweak" were practical or psychological has since been debated. What is not up for discussion is what happened. The Wildcats lost to Florida by one point in the closing seconds of the finals of the SEC Tournament and then roared their way to the national championship game. Along the way they beat undefeated Wichita State and defending champion Louisville.

As John Calipari's good idea changed his 2013-14 team, the good ideas we have shape our lives for the better. You've probably had a few moments of inspiration, divine or otherwise, yourself. Attending UK or becoming a Wildcat fan, marrying that person you did, maybe going back to school or starting a business or a family — they were good ideas.

From climbing aboard a horse's back to anesthesia to Double Stuf Oreos, good ideas are nothing new. The trouble is they're usually pretty hard to come by — except for the one that is right there before us all.

That woman with the bleeding problem had it. So did Jarius, the synagogue ruler. They had a big problem in their lives, so they came up with the notion that they should turn to Jesus and trust in him for help, hope, and deliverance.

It was a good idea then; it's a good idea now, the best ever, in fact. Surrendering your life to Jesus is such a good idea that its effects reverberate through all eternity.

I messed this up. Make me look good now.
— John Calipari to his team after his good idea

**Good ideas are hard to come by except for
the best idea of all: giving your life to Jesus.**

HAVE COURAGE

Read 1 Corinthians 16:13-14.

"Be on your guard; stand firm in the faith; be men of courage; be strong" (v. 13).

I shouldn't have done this," Feleica Stewart repeatedly told her husband before the Senior Night celebration of March 5, 2003. But she had the courage to do "this."

The night belonged to UK's three seniors — Keith Bogans, Jules Camara, and Marquis Estill — who were honored with video tributes and framed UK jerseys as they were joined by their parents on the court for the traditional pregame ceremony.

A fourth pair of parents, John and Feleica Stewart, joined the honorees at midcourt, but their son, John III, was not there with them. They were on hand to take part in a "lump-in-your-throat moment that forever will set apart this Senior Night from the others." John III could well have joined the Wildcat trio on this night since he had committed to Kentucky. He died, however, in a high school state playoff game in 1999.

Thus, the Stewarts gathered their courage and participated in a tearful Senior Night in which their son was recognized along with his would-be classmates. "As badly as John wanted to play basketball here, it would have been an injustice for us not to come," said Feleica. She also admitted that she considered leaving before she walked onto the court with her husband. "I shouldn't have done this," she kept saying.

WILDCATS

Fighting through her tears, she made it to midcourt where she was embraced by head coach Tubby Smith, the three seniors, and their families. The parents both broke into tears as they watched a video of their son's high-school exploits. They weren't alone. "This was the most moving senior ceremony I've been a part of," Smith said.

On a night when memories were made and courage was shown, the second-ranked Cats buried Vanderbilt 106-44.

When we speak of courage, we usually think of heroic actions such as that displayed by soldiers during wartime or firefighters during an inferno. But as Feleica and John Stewart demonstrated on Senior Night, there is another aspect to courage.

Like them, what makes our daily lives courageous isn't the absence of fear, which usually results either from foolhardiness or a dearth of relevant information. Rather, courage more often reveals itself in our determined refusal to let fear debilitate us.

This is the courage God calls upon us to demonstrate in our faith lives. When Paul urged the Christians in Corinth to "be men of courage," he wasn't telling them to rush into burning buildings. He was admonishing them to be strong and sure in their faith.

This courageous attitude is an absolute necessity for American Christians today when our faith is under attack as never before. Our spiritual courage reveals itself in our proclaiming the name of Jesus no matter what forces are arrayed against us.

It took a lot of courage for John and Feleica [Stewart] to do this.
— Tubby Smith on Senior Night

To be courageous for Jesus is to speak his name
boldly no matter what Satan uses against us.

FUN AND GAMES

Read Nehemiah 8:1-12.

"Do not grieve, for the joy of the Lord is your strength"
(v. 10c).

In preparation for their bowl game, the Cats balanced fun and work. The fun really began when the work was over and done.

UK head football coach Rich Brooks admitted that balancing fun and work leading up the 2006 Music City Bowl in Nashville was a struggle. Since the Cats were big underdogs to the Clemson Tigers, they had their work cut out for them.

But, hey, this was Music City, and there was much to do for the fun of it. There was the welcome party, for instance, that featured a rib-eating competition and a karaoke contest. There was the Fellowship of Christian Athletes breakfast. And then there were all the organized visits to places such as the Grand Ole Opry.

Even the practice field wasn't off limits to the fun. On Dec. 26, at their first practice in Nashville, some of the players swapped jerseys as a sort of day-after-Christmas celebration. Wide receiver Keenan Burton wore running back Rafael Little's No. 22 jersey, and Little donned Burton's No. 19. "A lot of people wanted to join the bandwagon," Burton said.

"I'm all for them having fun," Brooks warned his team, "but when they're on the practice field, they should be all business." Cat quarterback Andre Woodson got it. "I think the guys know when to turn it on and turn it off," he said about all the activities

WILDCATS

and the fun surrounding the game.

The whole UK team understood that the real fun lay in winning the game. Woodson threw three TD passes, including a 70-yarder to DeMoreo Ford, as Kentucky beat Clemson 28-20.

Now that was fun!

An erroneous stereotype of the Christian lifestyle has emerged over the centuries: that of a dour, sour-faced person always on the prowl to sniff out fun and frivolity and shut it down. "Somewhere, sometime, somebody's having fun — and it's got to stop!" Many understand this to be the mandate that governs the Christian life.

But even the Puritans, from whom that American stereotype largely comes, had parties, wore bright colors, and allowed their children to play games.

God's attitude toward fun is clearly illustrated by Nehemiah's instructions to the Israelites after Ezra had read them God's commandments. They broke out into tears because they had failed God, but Nehemiah told them not to cry but to eat, drink, and be merry instead. Go have fun, believers! Celebrate God's goodness and forgiveness!

This is still our mandate today because a life spent in an awareness of God's presence is all about celebrating, rejoicing, and enjoying God's countless gifts, especially salvation in Jesus Christ. To live for Jesus is to truly know the fun in living.

We've got to have fun when it's time for fun, and have football when it's time for football.
— Rich Brooks leading up to the Music City Bowl

What on God's wonderful Earth can be more fun that living for Jesus?

DAY 66

HOW YOU SEE IT

Read John 20:11-18.

"Mary stood outside the tomb crying" (v. 11).

Roger Newman had a different perspective on basketball than most. He was so little consumed by it that he left the UK team for academics and simply ignored two pro teams who drafted him.

A rugged 6-foot-4 forward, Newman averaged 16.1 points for the UK freshman team of 1956-57. Stardom was a sure thing. And then he left the program and his scholarship to concentrate on academics. His reason was simple: "In college I discovered I liked the academic side of things a great deal." The most surprising aspect of his decision to him was that a lot of folks who were so interested in him when he played basketball no longer were. "It's a rather rude awakening, I would say," he said.

Newman did, however, wind up playing basketball again for Big Blue. After a three-year layoff, he rejoined the team for the 1960-61 season as a fifth-year senior. His truce with Rupp was an unsteady one since the coach "didn't take kindly to basketball players who weren't consumed by basketball." That certainly included Newman.

He stayed in shape during his long layoff by playing for a YMCA team in Lexington that played freshman teams from area colleges. UK assistant coach Harry Lancaster let Newman know in January 1960 that they needed a player, and Newman rejoined the team. He was all set to play against Georgia Tech when the

SEC decided he couldn't play because of his YMCA competition.

Thus, Newman waited to join the team in the fall of 1960. He led the team in rebounds at 9.5 per game and finished second in scoring at 14.2 points per game. He set an NCAA record by hitting 17 free throws in the '61 regional game against Ohio State.

Newman's perspective about basketball didn't include just Kentucky. The Boston Celtics drafted him in 1960, and he didn't even bother showing up for training camp. He did the same thing to the Syracuse Nationals when they drafted him in '61.

Your perspective goes a long way toward determining whether you slink through life amid despair, anger, and hopelessness or stride boldly through life with joy and hope.

Mary Magdalene is an excellent example. On that first Easter morning, she stood by Jesus' tomb crying, her heart broken, because she still viewed everything through the perspective of Jesus' death. But how her attitude, her heart, and her life changed when she saw the morning through the perspective of Jesus' resurrection.

So it is with life and death for all of us. You can't avoid death, but you can determine how you perceive it. Is it fearful, dark, fraught with peril and uncertainty? Or is it a simple little passageway to glory, the light, and loved ones, an elevator ride to paradise?

It's a matter of perspective that depends totally on whether or not you're standing by Jesus' side when it arrives.

I think I have maybe a different perspective than most people.
— Roger Newman

**Whether death is your worst enemy or
a solicitous chauffeur is a matter of perspective.**

CELEBRATION TIME

Read Luke 15:1-10.

"There is rejoicing in the presence of the angels of God over one sinner who repents" (v. 10).

We'll celebrate later." So declared Victoria Dunlap before the 2011 NCAA Tournament. And so the Wildcats did.

Dunlap capped off her storied collegiate career in 2011 by becoming the first UK women's player ever taken in the first round of the WNBA. A 6-foot-1 forward, Dunlap was twice the SEC Player of the Year. She is Kentucky's second-leading scorer with 1,846 points, behind only Valerie Still. She is the first player in UK history with more than 300 steals, 100 assists, and 100 blocks. As a senior in 2011, she was the only player in the SEC to rank in the top five in scoring, rebounding, blocked shots, and steals.

She led the Wildcats to a berth in the NCAA Tournament and was so loose about the whole thing that at a news conference before the Cats' opening-round game, she suddenly burst into song. There was a method to her crooning, however. Her impromptu song was "Happy Birthday to You," sung to sophomore A'dia Mathies, who turned 20 that day, the eve of the UK game against 13th-seeded Hampton.

Dunlap finished "her pitch-perfect rendition." Then, as if reminding her teammates and herself where they were and what they were about, she said to Mathies, "We'll celebrate later."

She was right to turn serious. The 24-8 Cats had their hands full against the 25-6 Lady Pirates, who hit two late three-pointers and made a defensive stop to force the game into overtime.

It was the Wildcat defense, however, that owned the OT, forcing Hampton into missing its first five shots. Brittany Henderson scored the first four points of the extra period to propel the Cats toward their 66-62 win.

Dunlap's "later" time for celebration had come.

Kentucky just won another NCAA Tournament game. You got that new job or that promotion. You just held your newborn child in your arms. Life has those grand moments that call for celebration. You may jump up and down and scream in a wild frenzy at Rupp Arena or share a quiet, sedate candlelight dinner at home — but you celebrate.

Consider then a celebration that is beyond our imagining, one that fills every niche and corner of the very home of God and the angels. Imagine a celebration in Heaven, which also has its grand moments.

Those grand moments are touched off when someone comes to faith in Jesus. Heaven itself rings with the joyous sounds of the singing and dancing of the celebrating angels. Even God rejoices when just one person — you or someone you have introduced to Christ — turns to him.

When you said "yes" to Christ, you made the angels dance.

When it comes to celebrating, act like you've been there before.
— Terry Bowden

God himself joins the angels in heavenly celebration when even a single person turns to him through faith in Jesus.

DAY 68

WHAT A SURPRISE!

Read 1 Thessalonians 5:1-11.

"But you, brothers, are not in darkness so that this day should surprise you like a thief" (v. 4).

Imagine the surprise when Washington and Lee's basketball team showed up for a game Kentucky officials, coaches, and players didn't even know was scheduled.

The Wildcats of head coach Ray Eklund were a sterling 15-3 in 1925-26. The squad featured the university's second All-America, guard Burgess Carey. He was a defensive specialist whom fellow team captain James McFarland called, "big and tough and strong. . . . He would just slam into guys." Burgess seldom went beyond midcourt and very rarely shot the ball.

After starting the season with a pair of losses, the Cats reeled off seven straight wins, the last a 46-19 thumping of Centre in Danville on Thursday, Feb. 4. The Cats were going about their business on Friday, Feb. 5, when to their surprise, the Washington and Lee basketball team showed up, having come all the way from Lexington, Va. The team manager produced a signed contract proving that the game was on for that night. Apparently, UK officials had either overlooked or forgotten about the game.

Eklund took the unusual measure of rounding up his players and putting them to bed for an afternoon nap. Meanwhile, Athletic Director S.A. Boles assembled the university band and had them parade through the streets of Lexington to advertise the night's surprise. "The blare of trumpets did its work"; more than 2,500 persons turned out for the game.

Apparently still surprised at having to play, UK trailed 22-20 at halftime. The Cats vaulted into a 32-24 lead early into the last half, though, and pulled away for a 44-34 win behind 19 points from Gayle Mohney, who was also a star quarterback on the football team. Forward Paul Jenkins had a dozen points.

Surprise birthday parties are a delight. And what's the fun of opening Christmas presents when we already know what's in them? Some surprises in life provide us with experiences that are both joyful and delightful.

Generally, though, we expend energy and resources to avoid most surprises and the impact they may have upon our lives. We may be surprised by the exact timing of a baby's arrival, but we nevertheless have the bags packed beforehand and the nursery all set for its occupant. Paul used this very image (v. 3) to describe the Day of the Lord, when Jesus will return to claim his own and establish his kingdom. We may be caught by surprise, but we must still be ready.

The consequences of being caught unprepared by a baby's insistence on being born are serious indeed. They pale, however, beside the eternal effects of not being ready when Jesus returns. We prepare ourselves just as Paul told us to (v. 8): We live in faith, hope, and love, ever on the alert for that great, promised day.

Surprise me.
   — *Yogi Berra to his wife on where she should bury him*

The timing of Jesus' return will be a surprise; the consequences should not be.

GOOD ADVICE

Read Isaiah 9:1-7.

"And he will be called Wonderful Counselor" (v. 6b).

Adolph Rupp didn't like the advice he got, but he took it and won a national championship.

Wallace "Wah Wah" Jones was one of the university's greatest athletes. He won four varsity letters in football and basketball and three in baseball and is the only UK athlete to have his number retired in both basketball and football.

In 1947, his sophomore season, Jones decided to give up football to concentrate on basketball, but head coach Bear Bryant would have none of that and persuaded Jones to change his mind. Late in the season, though, Jones injured his ankle and was late reporting for basketball practice. "Rupp was always using football against me," he recalled, and Rupp did it again. The coach claimed Jones wasn't in good basketball shape and refused to play him.

Early that season the team made an eastern road trip. On the road, Rupp would retire to his hotel room, don his favorite red pajamas, and then summon someone to his room to socialize and talk basketball. After Temple beat the Cats 60-59, Rupp called for the team manager, Humzey Yessin, who was a former high-school teammate of Jones', to come up and talk with him.

He asked Yessin what he thought was wrong with his team, and in reply, the manager offered him some advice.: "We'll start playing better when you get Wah Wah back in the starting lineup."

Rupp countered that the manager was just showing favoritism toward his old friend.

The next night, though, Jones was in the lineup against St. John's and UK won. Jones started every game the rest of the season, and the team went 36-3 and won the NCAA championship.

We all need a little advice now and then. More often than not, we turn to professional counselors, who are all over the place. Grief counselors, marriage counselors, school guidance counselors, rehabilitation counselors, all sorts of mental health and addiction counselors — We even have pet counselors. No matter what our situation or problem, we can find plenty of advice for the taking.

The problem, of course, is that we find advice easy to offer but hard to take. We also have a rueful tendency to solicit the wrong source for advice, seeking counsel that doesn't really solve our problem but that instead enables us to continue with it.

Our need for outside advice, for an independent perspective on our situation, is actually God-given. God serves many functions in our lives, but one role clearly delineated in his Word is that of Counselor. Jesus himself is described as the "Wonderful Counselor." All the advice we need in our lives is right there for the asking; we don't even have to pay for it except with our faith. God is always there for us: to listen, to lead, and to guide.

I don't think you want to listen to what the fans say. If you listen to them too much, you'll be sitting up there with them.
— Va. Tech football coach Frank Beamer on taking advice from fans

We all need and seek advice in our lives,
but the ultimate and most wonderful Counselor
is of divine and not human origin.

STRANGE BUT TRUE

Read Philippians 2:1-11.

"And being found in appearance as a man, he humbled himself and became obedient to death — even death on a cross!" (v. 8)

It's strange but true: UK once played a game in which the two teams punted more times than they ran plays from scrimmage.

Kentucky head coach Chet Wynne (1934-37) said one time that "the punt was football's most important and efficient weapon." Thus, he conducted a thorough search to replace Ralph Kercheval (1931-33), who remains a Kentucky and college football legend. Kercheval had a 77-yard punt in the 7-6 win over Georgia Tech in 1933 that stood as the school record until 1983.

In the 7-2 win over Florida in '33, John Simms "Shipwreck" Kelly (See Devotion No. 9.) recalled that with UK leading in the closing seconds and sitting at its own 20, he told team captain Ralph "Babe" Wright he wanted to see Kercheval kick one more time. So Wright called a punt, and Kercheval kicked the ball out of the stadium and into the bay. "That is the only time I've ever seen a ball kicked out of a stadium," Kelly said.

Wynne finally settled on Bert Johnson, a triple-threat star who was UK's second All-SEC performer (after Kercheval), to punt in 1934. On Sept. 29, 1934, Kentucky and Washington & Lee met in what turned out to be one of the strangest football games ever played. "The mud was knee deep that day," Johnson recalled. "All we did all afternoon was kick." The refs kept using the same ball, wiping it off and sending it back in, and "it was like kicking a brick, almost."

Neither team wanted to keep the ball because they couldn't do anything with it. So they punted. An incredible 70 times, 36 for UK. The Cats didn't run a play from scrimmage in the third quarter and ran only 22 the entire game to W&L's 24.

Perhaps not strange at all about the game is that the only score was set up by a blocked punt as W&L won 7-0.

Life is just strange. How else can we explain tofu, that people go to bars hoping to meet the "right" person, the proliferation of tattoos, and the behavior of teenagers? Isn't it strange that someone would hear the life-changing, affirming message of salvation through Jesus Christ and then walk away from it?

And how strange is God's plan to save us? He could have come roaring down, destroying and blasting everyone whose sinfulness offended him, which, of course, is pretty much all of us. Then he could have brushed off his hands, nodded the divine head, and left a scorched planet in his wake. All in a day's work.

Instead, God came up with a totally novel plan: He would save the world by becoming a human being, letting himself be humiliated, tortured, and killed, and thus establishing a kingdom of justice and righteousness that will last forever.

It's a strange way to save the world — but it's true.

Seventy times that grimy, slippery football sailed into the air.
— Writer Russell Rice on the strange game with W&L in 1934

**It's strange but true: God allowed himself
to be killed on a cross to save the world.**

DAY 71

WANT ADS

Read Psalm 73:23-28.

"Whom have I in heaven but you? And earth has nothing I desire besides you" (v. 25).

Lousville got exactly the kind of game it wanted against the Wildcats. Unfortunately for the Cardinals, so did Michael Kidd-Gilchrist.

Prior to the Battle for the Bluegrass on Dec. 31, 2011, UK head coach John Calipari "did everything but hire an airplane to circle Rupp Arena towing a banner" to get across his message that the game would be "a push-shove-slugfest . . . physical to the extreme."

The boss Cat knew it was coming because Louisville's roster couldn't match up with Kentucky's. Thus, head coach Rick Pitino wanted a slower, physical game — and that's what he got. The game was played "down on basketball's mean streets, with plenty of elbows and forearms and shrieking whistles." Apparently trying to keep the game from devolving into a brawl, the zebras called 52 fouls that resulted in 70 free throws. Calipari landed a technical for arguing that *not enough* fouls were being called.

So if Louisville got what it wanted, did the Cardinals upset the 12-1 Cats? Uh, no. Kentucky prevailed 69-62, largely because Kidd-Gilchrist flourished amid all the mayhem.

"He wasn't bothered as much as some of the others by the physical play," Calipari said of his freshman forward. He played 39 minutes, scored 24 points, and grabbed 19 rebounds. After all,

WILDCATS

receiving some hard knocks wasn't new for the 6-foot-7 star. He had to overcome a childhood stutter. His father was killed when he was 2 years old. His uncle died on the day he was to sign his letter-of-intent to UK. His mother had recently been hospitalized.

From New Jersey, Kidd-Gilchrist admitted he knew little about the intensity of the rivalry. "I just wanted to win the game," he said. Which the Cats did. Along with 37 others that storied season, setting an NCAA record on the way to the national title.

What do you want out of life? A loving family, a home of your own, the respect of those whom you admire? Our heart's desires can elevate us to greatness and goodness, but they can also plunge us into destruction, despair, and evil. Drugs, alcohol, control, sex, power, worldly success: Do these desires motivate you?

Desires are not inherently evil or bad for you; after all, God planted the capacity to desire in us. The key is determining which of your heart's desires are healthful and are worth pursuing and which are dangerous and are best avoided.

Not surprisingly, the answer to the dilemma lies with God. You consult the one whose own heart's desire is for what is unequivocally best for you, who is driven only by his unqualified love for you. You match what you want for yourself with what God wants for you. Your deepest heart's desire must be the establishment and maintenance of an intimate relationship with God.

I'm built for this. I just love the challenge.
— Michael Kidd-Gilchrist on the physical Louisville game

Whether our desires drive us to greatness
or to destruction is determined by
whether they are also God's desires for our lives.

DAY 72

BIG DEAL

Read Ephesians 3:1-13.

"His intent was that now, through the church, the manifold wisdom of God should be made known" (v. 10).

What the Wildcats did to the LSU Tigers on Oct. 13, 2007, was one really big deal.

On that date, Kentucky pulled off one of the biggest wins in school history by outlasting undefeated and top-ranked LSU 43-37 in three overtimes. The win was UK's first over a No.-1 team since a 27-21 defeat of Mississippi in 1964.

While admitting the win was one of the biggest in his career that started in 1977, head coach Rich Brooks refused to call the win a huge upset. "I just like to think that . . . if we play well enough, we can beat any team in the nation," he said.

The Tigers seemed to be on their way to a spotless 7-0 record when they led 27-14 with 3:49 left in the third quarter. But the Cats scored on their next possession, quarterback Andre Woodson hitting senior tight end Jacob Tamme with an 8-yard TD toss. Lones Seiber completed the UK comeback with two fourth-quarter field goals that knotted the game at 27.

The comeback against the nation's top-ranked team was no surprise to Brooks. "I can't say enough about the character and the guts of this football team," he said.

When LSU missed a last-gasp 57-yard field goal, the game went into overtime. After both teams scored in the first OT, Seiber had

WILDCATS

to come through with a 43-yard kick to tie the game at 37 and send the game into a third overtime.

On third-and-goal- from the 7, Woodson let fly just before he was drilled, and wide receiver Steve Johnson hauled the pass in at the goal line. When LSU held on the two-point conversion try, the door was open for a Tiger win.

UK linebacker Braxton Kelly slammed it shut when he dropped an LSU back on fourth-and-two short of the first down.

"Big deals" such as that Wildcat win over LSU are important components of the unfolding of our lives. Our wedding, childbirth, a new job, a new house, big UK games, even a new car. In many ways, what we regard as a big deal is what shapes not only our lives but our character.

One of the most unfathomable anomalies of faith in America today is that while many people profess to be die-hard Christians, they disdain involvement with a local church. As Paul tells us, however, the Church is a very big deal to God; it is at the heart of his redemptive work; it is a vital part of his eternal purposes.

The Church is no accident of history. It isn't true that Jesus died and all he wound up with for his troubles was the stinking Church. It is no consolation prize.

Rather, the church is the primary instrument through which God's plan of cosmic and eternal salvation is worked out. And it doesn't get any bigger than that.

It's got to be right up there at the top.
— Rich Brooks on how big the win over LSU was

To disdain church involvement is to assert that God doesn't know what he's doing.

TIME FOR A CHANGE

Read Romans 6:1-14.

"Just as Christ was raised from the dead through the glory of the Father, we too may live a new life" (v. 4).

Rick Pitino changed his star's position twice in a week, and UK wound up with another national championship.

Tony Delk was destined for stardom when he arrived in Lexington in 1992, and everyone knew it, including Pitino. The head coach decided, though, that stardom for Delk lay in moving from shooting guard to point guard.

Delk later admitted that playing point guard was a much bigger challenge than he had anticipated. But he did his best, working hard and leaning on guard Travis Ford for help.

Pitino changed his mind about Delk before the 1993-94 season began. In the opening game, the sophomore was in the starting lineup for the first time. More importantly for Delk, he was on the court as the shooting guard and not as the "dreaded" point guard.

That's where Delk stayed for the next two seasons, and he became the star everyone had expected. He led the Cats in scoring both seasons and was Third-Team All- America his junior season.

When Delk's senior season of 1995-96 arrived, Pitino changed his mind again, though he made the move to benefit his senior's pro career: He moved Delk back to point guard. Explaining the move, Pitino said the position change would allow Delk to improve his ball-handling skills, "which should enable him to be a first-round draft pick."

As he had as a freshman, though, Delk struggled at the position. When the Cats lost to UMass in the second game of the season, Pitino made another change: He scrapped his previous change, moving Delk back to shooting guard.

The result was Wildcat legend. Delk was First-Team All-America and Kentucky won its sixth national championship. After the season, Pitino admitted that had he not made the change in the backcourt, UK probably wouldn't have won the title.

Anyone who asserts no change is needed in his or her life just isn't paying attention. Every life has doubt, worry, fear, failure, frustration, unfulfilled dreams, and unsuccessful relationships in some combination. The memory and consequences of our past often haunt and trouble us.

Recognizing the need for change in our lives, though, doesn't mean the changes that will bring about hope, joy, peace, and fulfillment will occur. We need some power greater than ourselves or we wouldn't be where we are.

So where can we turn to? Where lies the hope for a changed life? It lies in an encounter with the Lord of all Hope: Jesus Christ. For a life turned over to Jesus, change is inevitable. With Jesus in charge, the old self with its painful and destructive ways of thinking, feeling, loving, and living is transformed.

A changed life is always only a talk with Jesus away.

Change is an essential element of sports, as it is of life.
— *Erik Brady*, USA Today

**In Jesus lie the hope and the power
that change lives.**

THE LEADER

Read Matthew 16:18-23.

"You are Peter, and on this rock I will build my church, and the gates of Hades will not overcome it" (v. 18).

Head coach Tubby Smith basically had one word for his sophomore point guard: Lead. The immediate result was a memorable game; the long-range result was an NCAA berth.

The Wildcats of 2005-06 were struggling in the early going. They were ranked 23rd in the nation, but they were only 6-3 and had lost a couple of high-profile games. Sophomore point guard Rajon Rondo wasn't playing badly. After all, against Iowa on Nov. 21, he had set a school record for a point guard with 19 rebounds. But still, something was missing from his game and from the team; Smith knew exactly what it was.

So he called Rondo into his office for what turned out to be a frank, 45-minute talk. The coach's message for Rondo was simple: It was time for him to step up and be a leader for his team. Like his coach, Rondo was ready for the meeting. "We knew it was time for us to talk," he said. "I walked out of there knowing that Coach has a lot of confidence in me, and that made me feel good."

The meeting came just in time; up next for the Cats were the 4th-ranked Louisville Cardinals. Before the third-largest crowd in Rupp Arena history, Rondo showed he had taken the meeting to heart. With a newfound bounce in his step and a new demeanor on the court, he led the Cats to a 73-61 smashing of the Cards.

WILDCATS

He scored a career-high 25 points, but that wasn't the most important aspect of his game that night. "He was like a captain out there, like a general," said guard Ravi Moss. "He's the guy who got us going," agreed fellow guard Ramel Bradley.

Rondo's leadership proved crucial all season long as the Cats went on to earn a berth in the NCAA Tournament.

Every aspect of life that involves people — every organization, every group, every project, every team — must have a leader. If goals are to be reached, somebody must take charge.

Even the early Christian church was no different. Jesus knew this, so he designated the leader in Simon Peter, who was such an unlikely choice to assume such an awesome, world-changing responsibility that Jesus soon after rebuked him as "Satan."

In *Twelve Ordinary Men*, John MacArthur described Simon as "ambivalent, vacillating, impulsive, unsubmissive." Hardly a man to inspire confidence in his leadership skills. Yet, according to MacArthur, Peter became "the greatest preacher among the apostles" and the "dominant figure" in the birth of the church.

The implication for your own life is both obvious and unsettling. You may think you lack the attributes necessary to make a good leader for Christ. But consider Simon Peter, an ordinary man who allowed Christ to rule his life and became the foundation upon which the Christian church was built.

Leadership, like coaching, is fighting for the hearts and souls of men and getting them to believe in you.
— Legendary college coach Eddie Robinson

God's leaders are men and women who allow Jesus to lead them.

DAY 75

ONE TOUGH COOKIE

Read 2 Corinthians 11:21b-29.

"Besides everything else, I face daily the pressure of my concern for all the churches" (v. 28).

Football is a tough sport for tough men, but few in UK history can match Curtis Sanders for toughness.

Called "a virtual iron man," Sanders, one of UK's greatest full-backs, "averaged almost 60 minutes a game for four years, playing in constant pain from midway through his sophomore season until his final game in 1924." He "played five games with a broken right hand in a cast, had his nose broken four times, played with both shoulders separated, had bones chipped in both ankles, and kept right on tackling despite damaged cartilage and vertebrae in his neck."

When trainer Frank Mann suggested Sanders would be wise to give up football, he replied that he couldn't let his buddies down. Decades later, Sanders said he was knocked unconscious in every game of his senior year. According to Sanders, "They made me a special helmet with heavy straps across the top on the inside so my head wouldn't touch the helmet."

Missing in those early days of college football were any sophisticated training techniques or equipment. "I remember the trainer did a lot of massaging of bruises," Sanders said. "He had an infra-red machine. I 'cooked' those shoulders in the shower, and that was our 'whirlpool.'" The only precaution Sanders took was taping

WILDCATS

his ankles before every game. "We never thought about playing without tape," he said.

Sanders also required special equipment in 1922 for his separated shoulders. "I couldn't raise my arms above my eyes without pain," he remembered. Armed with two heavy, stiff pads laced together, he could barely move his arms at all.

But tough cookie that he was, he played on.

You don't have to be a legendary Kentucky fullback to be tough. In America today, toughness isn't restricted to physical accomplishments and brute strength. Going to work every morning even when you feel bad, sticking by your rules for your children in a society that ridicules parental authority, making hard decisions about your aging parents' care often over their objections — you've got to be tough every day just to live honorably, decently, and justly.

Living faithfully requires toughness, too, though in America chances are you won't be imprisoned, stoned, or flogged this week for your faith as Paul was. Still, contemporary society exerts subtle, psychological, daily pressures on you to turn your back on your faith and your values. Popular culture promotes promiscuity, atheism, and gutter language; your children's schools have kicked God out; the corporate culture advocates amorality before the shrine of the almighty dollar.

You have to hang tough to keep the faith.

Sandy, if you had any brains, you'd quit.
— UK trainer Frank Mann to Curtis Sanders

Life demands more than mere physical toughness; you must be spiritually tough too.

NOT WHAT THEY SEEM

Read Habakkuk 1:2-11.

"Why do you make me look at injustice? Why do you tolerate wrong? Destruction and violence are before me; there is strife, and conflict abounds" (v. 3).

The newspapers told of Adolph Rupp's brilliant coaching move that resulted in a last-second win for the Wildcats. Ah, but things weren't quite what they seemed.

On Dec. 31, 1963, Rupp's second-ranked Wildcats took on No.-8 Duke in the championship game of the Sugar Bowl Tournament in New Orleans. UK was led by the legendary Cotton Nash, who had his usual game, pouring in 30 points.

The game seesawed back and forth as everyone expected. The score was tied at 79 when Kentucky's defensive specialist, Tom Kron, stole the ball and the Wildcats called a time out with seven seconds to play. Everybody in the gym expected Nash to take the shot. Instead, junior guard Terry Mobley — who, as Nash put it, "hadn't done much" — banked in a 13-foot shot for the winner.

The next morning, the headline of a New Orleans newspaper proclaimed, "Rupp Surprises Duke; Calls on Mobley to Take the Winning Shot." Actually, that's not the way it was at all.

Rupp did exactly what everyone — including Duke — expected: He set up a play that called for Nash to take the shot. But, Nash said, "The defense really kept me covered." As a result, Mobley, who had scored seven points in the game, found himself open with the ball and time running out. "I really had no choice but to shoot it," he said.

Rupp then did something he had never done before: He ran onto the court to congratulate Mobley, running straight toward him. He had an ulterior motive, though as he quickly told Mobley, "Remember. We knew Duke was expecting Nash to get the ball, so we outsmarted them and instructed you to take the last shot."

Thus, Mobley had the last shot and Rupp had the last laugh.

Just as with basketball, in life things sometime aren't what they seem. In our violent and convulsive times, we must confront the possibility of a new reality: that we are helpless in the face of anarchy; that injustice, destruction, and violence are pandemic in and symptomatic of our modern age. Anarchy seems to be winning, and the system of standards, values, and institutions we have cherished appears to be crumbling while we watch.

But we should not be deceived or disheartened. God is in fact the arch-enemy of chaos, the creator of order and goodness and the architect of all of history. God is in control. We often misinterpret history as the record of mankind's accomplishments — which it isn't — rather than the unfolding of God's plan — which it is. That plan has a clearly defined end: God will make everything right. In that day things will be what they seem.

[Terry] Mobley may have been the last Wildcat the Blue Devils expected to take the vital shot.
— Courier-Journal *on the '63 Duke game*

**The forces of good and decency often seem
helpless before evil's power, but don't be fooled:
God is in control and will set things right.**

DAY 77

TEN TO REMEMBER

Read Exodus 20:1-17.

*"God spoke all these words: 'I am the Lord your God . . . .
You shall have no other gods before me'" (vv. 1, 3).*

Sam Bowie, Kevin Grevey, Rex Chapman, and Louie Dampier. Just four of the UK greats who didn't make the top ten on a list of the greatest basketball players in Wildcat history.

In January 2011, Dan Bodner of *bleacherreport.com* chose UK's 25 best players ever. No. 10 on his list is Kyle Macy (1977-80), the first Wildcat to be named the SEC Player of the Year and still UK's all-time leader in career free-throw percentage (89%). No. 9 on the list is Ralph Beard (1945-49), Kentucky's first four-time All-SEC selection and a three- time All-America who led the "Fab Five" to back-to-back national titles. According to Bodner, the No. 8 player is Alex Groza (1944-49), who is also a member of the "Fab Five" and a three-time All-America.

No. 7 is Tony Delk (1992-96), who holds the school career mark for most three pointers (283). The sixth greatest player on the list is Kenny "Sky" Walker (1982-86). He was All-SEC four times, All-America twice, and the SEC Player of the Year twice. He is second on the Kentucky all-time scoring list.

Bodner chose Cotton Nash (1961-64) as the fifth greatest player in UK history. He was All-SEC and All-America each of his three seasons in Lexington. No. 4 on Bodner's list is Jack Givens (1974-78), who is perhaps best remembered for the 41 points he hung on

Duke in the national championship game of 1978.

Wallace "Wah Wah" Jones (1945-49) is No. 3. (See Devotion No. 69.) The second greatest player in program history is Jamal Mashburn (1990-93), who "almost single-handedly altered UK's history" as the "first blue chip player to sign with Kentucky after the program had endured a very dark probation period."

And No. 1? Dan Issel (1966-70), who still stands as UK's all-time leading scorer (2,138 points) and rebounder (1,078).

For UK fans, these are indeed ten to remember for the ages.

You've got your list and you're ready to go: a gallon of paint and a water hose from the hardware store; chips, peanuts, and sodas from the grocery store for watching tonight's UK game; the tickets for the band concert. Your list helps you remember.

God also made a list once of things he wanted you to remember; it's called the Ten Commandments. Just as your list reminds you to do something, so does God's list remind you of how you are to act in your dealings with other people and with him.

A life dedicated to Jesus is a life devoted to relationships, and God's list emphasizes that the social life and the spiritual life of the faithful cannot be sundered. God's relationship to you is one of unceasing, unqualified love, and you are to mirror that divine love in your relationships with others. In case you forget, you have a list.

Society today treats the Ten Commandments as if they were the ten suggestions. Never compromise on right or wrong.
— Former college baseball coach Gordie Gillespie

God's list is a set of instructions on how you are to conduct yourself with other people and with him.

LESSON LEARNED

Read Psalm 143.

"Teach me to do your will, for you are my God" (v. 10).

Bear Bryant learned a lesson from the 1951 Orange Bowl, and the result was a Kentucky win in the '52 Sugar Bowl.

Bryant coached the Wildcats from 1946-53. His sixty wins remain the most of any UK coach in history, and his winning percentage of .710 is the best of any coach since before the World War I era. His 1950 team won the school's first SEC title.

That 10-1 season of 1950 earned the Cats a berth in the Orange Bowl. Always one to work his team hard, Bryant didn't let up for the bowl game. The team went straight to the practice field upon its arrival in hot Cocoa Beach. More than a dozen guys passed out during a two-hour practice; Bryant simply kept moving his team around to avoid the bodies.

Each day, the head coach practiced the team in full pads morning and afternoon in the broiling sun and the sand. Team trainer Smokey Harper warned Bryant that he was exhausting the team, but the coach didn't listen.

Meanwhile, Santa Clara, the opposition, made a leisurely trip from California, stopping several times to enjoy the scenery.

Kentucky led 7-0 at halftime but folded in the last half and lost 21-13. After the game, Bryant told his team, "Boys, hold your heads up. It's my fault. I just worked you too hard."

But the coach had learned his lesson. Next year on the way to the Sugar Bowl, Bryant put his team through a week of workouts in Mobile, gave them a short layoff, and then held workouts for a week in Baton Rouge. "We practiced only an hour and a half in shorts each morning and not near so long in pads in the afternoon," said star halfback/safety Emery Clark.

This time, the Wildcats pulled off one of the greatest upsets in school history. They snapped Oklahoma's 31-game win streak with a 13-7 win.

Learning about anything in life requires a combination of education and experience. Education is the accumulation of facts that we call knowledge; experience is the acquisition of wisdom and discernment, which add purpose and understanding to our knowledge.

The most difficult way to learn is trial and error: dive in blindly and mess up. The best way to learn is through example coupled with a set of instructions: Someone has gone ahead to show you the way and has written down all the information you need to follow.

In teaching us the way to live godly lives, God chose the latter method. He set down in his book the habits, actions, and attitudes that make for a way of life in accordance with his wishes. He also sent us Jesus to explain and to illustrate.

God teaches us not only how to exist but how to live. We just need to be attentive students.

Bryant told us he had learned something at Cocoa.
— Emery Clark on the 1952 Sugar Bowl

To learn from Jesus is to learn what life is all about and how God means for us to live it.

THE FAME GAME

Read 1 Kings 10:1-10, 18-29.

"King Solomon was greater in riches and wisdom than all the other kings of the earth. The whole world sought audience with Solomon" (vv. 23-24).

They may well be the UK national champs nobody's heard of.

In 2011, the most successful Kentucky athletic program this side of men's basketball won the NCAA national championship. That would be the university's rifle team. The national title was overdue for a program so good that since 1994 the team has never finished lower than ninth in the country and through 2014 has finished in the top three twelve times.

The architect of the program is head coach Harry Mullins, a fixture in the UK athletics department for more than thirty years. He was born in Germany, didn't speak English until he was 8, and didn't become an American citizen until he was 18. He started shooting as a teenager and enrolled at Kentucky in 1982 where he was a three-time SEC shooting champion. He graduated in 1987 and took over the rifle team the same year.

After finishing as the runners-up in 1997, 2001, 2002, and 2009, the Wildcats claimed the title in 2011 in a finish so close as to defy description. The team edged West Virginia by three points, 4700-4697. That amounted to a fraction of an inch spread out over two days of shooting. "Our lead was smaller than this," said Mullins, holding up a key chain that was only about a quarter of an inch thick. "And that's over 480 shots."

Five UK shooters earned All-America honors for the season: first-teamers Henri Junghanel and Emily Holsopple and second-teamers Logan Fox, Heather Greathouse, and Ethan Settlemires, who was named Shooter of the Match for the championships.

Still, even though they were NCAA champs, they probably were never exactly famous on campus or elsewhere around town.

Have you ever wanted to be famous? Hanging out with other rich and famous people, having microphones capture your every word, throwing money around, signing autographs, and posing for the paparazzi before you climb into your imported sports car?

Many of us yearn to be famous, well-known in the places and by the people that we believe matter. That's all fame amounts to: strangers knowing your name and your face.

The truth is that you are already famous where it really does matter, which excludes TV's talking heads, screaming teenagers, rapt moviegoers, or D.C. power brokers. You are famous because Almighty God knows your name, your face, and everything else there is to know about you.

If a persistent photographer snapped you pondering this fame – the only kind that has eternal significance – would the picture reveal unbridled joy or a shell-shocked mug shot?

When you play a sport, you have two things in mind. One is to get into the Hall of Fame and the other is to go to heaven when you die.
— Golfer Lee Trevino

You're already famous
because God knows your name and your face,
which may be either reassuring or terrifying.

DAY 80

MERCY ME

Read Ephesians 2:1-10.

"Because of his great love for us, God, who is rich in mercy, made us alive with Christ even when we were dead in transgressions – it is by grace you have been saved" (vv. 4-5).

Because the league had in effect forced him to kick two All-Americas off his team, UK head man Adolph Rupp was in no position to show mercy had he even been inclined to do so.

Bob Brannum was the youngest All-America in UK basketball history. He graduated from high school at 16 and turned 17 in the summer of 1943 but was too young for the draft. Instead, he reported to Rupp in Lexington and was a first-team All-America in 1943-44. After he turned 18 in May, he was drafted. He returned to Lexington after the war, but found a whole bunch of Rupp recruits on hand and couldn't crack the lineup as a starter.

Jim Jordan had twice been All-America at North Carolina as a Navy V-12 student during the war. When he came to Lexington after the war, he, too, had trouble getting playing time.

Thus, when the SEC told Rupp to cut his roster from twelve to ten for the 1947 league tournament, the coach made what would seem to be a bizarre move: He booted two All-Americas, Brannum and Jordan, off the team. Two freshmen, Jim Line and Dale Barnstable, made the roster instead. "We'll need speed, not height, to win this affair," Rupp explained.

WILDCATS

The coach had earlier proposed to the league that the rosters be upped to twelve for the tournament, but his proposal was voted down seven to five, perhaps because it was Rupp who proposed it. Vanderbilt's coach was one of those voting against the idea.

The coach used the tournament to demonstrate how inane the rule was. Lacking two subs, he turned his firepower loose and showed no mercy, blasting Vandy 98-29 in the opening round.

A drunk slams into your car, injuring members of your family. A thug burglarizes your house. Your boss gives the promotion you deserve to someone else.

Somebody sometime in your life has hurt you. What's your attitude toward them? Do you scream for revenge and payback? Or do you extend mercy, showing compassion and kindness all out of proportion to what's been done to you?

Mercy is the appeal of last resort. When you are guilty, your only hope is to throw yourself upon the mercy of the court. Your only prayer is that the judge will not remorselessly hand down the sentence you deserve.

Of all God's attributes, none is more astounding than his penchant for mercy. Through Jesus, God has provided the way we may be saved from the sentence we deserve. Through Jesus, God made his divine mercy available to us all. In so doing, however, God expects that we who avail ourselves of his mercy will show mercy toward others. We reap what we sow.

There wasn't much Rupp could do. He only had ten players.
— Vandy head coach Norman Cooper

To sow mercy in our lifetimes is to reap mercy from God when we stand guiltily before him.

GOOD LUCK

Read Acts 1:15-25.

*"Then they prayed, 'Lord, you know everyone's heart.
Show us which of these two you have chosen.' . . . Then
they cast lots" (vv. 24, 25a).*

Sometimes sheer dumb luck bails a team out — even the Cats.

On Jan. 13, 2004, Kentucky took on Mississippi State in the SEC headliner and a game of national importance. Kentucky was 10-1 and ranked No. 5 while the 20th-ranked Bulldogs were 13-0. For the final 13 minutes of the last half, State was the better team on the floor, outscoring the smaller Cats 31-16 by pounding the backboards relentlessly.

The result was a comeback that seemed to have given the Dogs one of the biggest wins in school history. They led 66-65 with only 2.5 seconds on the clock as UK set up to inbounds the ball.

What happened made it seem "as if the Bulldogs had been in the Wildcats' huddle during the time out." And then luck came into play and sealed the deal for Big Blue.

Guard Gerald Fitch, whose hot shooting had been the catalyst behind the Cats' 18-point lead in the first half, came off a screen near the top of the key. As if they knew exactly what UK would do, two "possibly telepathic" Dogs were waiting for him.

Inbounding the ball from the sideline, Cliff Hawkins tried two fakes — including one to Fitch — before he ran out of options. He then heaved a desperate Hail Mary pass in the direction of for-

WILDCATS

ward Chuck Hayes near the basket.

Again, State was ready. A Dog defender and Hayes both got a hand on the ball, knocking it away. Right to senior forward Erik Daniels, "who was standing in the middle of the lane, as innocent a bystander as there's ever been." Uncontested, he laid it up and in at the buzzer for a 67-66 Wildcat win.

"We were a little lucky tonight," head coach Tubby Smith said in a rather classic example of understatement.

Ever think sometimes that other people have all the luck? Some guy wins a lottery while you can't get a raise of a few lousy bucks at work. The basketball takes a lucky bounce the other team's way and UK loses a game. If you have any luck to speak of, it's bad.

To ascribe anything that happens in life to blind luck, however, is to believe that random chance controls everything, including you. But here's the truth: There is no such thing as luck, good or bad. Even when the apostles in effect flipped a coin to pick the new guy, they acknowledged that the lots merely revealed to them a decision God had already made.

It's true that we can't explain why some people skate merrily through life while others suffer in horrifying ways. We don't know why good things happen to bad people and vice versa. But none of it results from luck, unless you want to attribute that name to the force that does indeed control the universe; you know — the one more commonly called God.

I'd rather be lucky than good, but I think we have a combination of both.
— Tubby Smith after the win over Miss. State

A force does exist that is in charge,
but it isn't luck; it's God.

BEING DIFFERENT

Read Daniel 3.

"We want you to know, O king, that we will not serve your gods or worship the image of gold you have set up" *(v. 18).*

Dicky Lyons, Sr. was — well, he was different. He was also one of the greatest players in Kentucky football history.

An all-purpose back, Lyons played at Kentucky from 1966-68. He was First-Team All-SEC as a junior and as a senior and was the first player in SEC history to amass 1,000 yards rushing, 1000 kickoff return yards, and 1,000 punt return yards.

Lyons "was known to commit interesting acts of violence." In a 1967 game, he decked a teammate for missing a block. In a pre-season scrimmage, he seethed as the coaches ordered a play run over and over because an end kept missing his block. Finally, he marched up to the repeat offender and dropped him with a fore-arm to the jaw. The player blocked his man on the next run. Once in practice when the fullback took his time getting into his stance, Lyons planted a knee in his backside, sending him sprawling on his face. "It's just kind of silly when you got 10 guys doin' the right thing and only one guy who is messin' up," Lyons explained.

In the '67 Vandy game, the bench called a quarterback sneak from in close. Lyons realized the Commodores must have heard the call because they put seven men on the line. He told his QB not to go ahead with the play and was told "Shut up, Lyons." Lyons then ordered the center, Kenny Woods, not to snap the ball. The quarterback went ahead with the snap count until Woods raised up and told him he wasn't snapping the ball. The quarterback called time out, changed the play, and Lyons scored. UK won 12-7.

Word had it that Lyons led the UK campus in unpaid parking tickets and was an inveterate player of the horses. He was different all right, but he was serious about his football — and good at it.

While we live in a secular society that constantly pressures us to conform to its principles and values, we serve a risen Christ who calls us to be different. Therein lies the great conflict of the Christian life in contemporary America.

But how many of us really consider that even in our secular society we struggle to conform? We are all geeks in a sense. We can never truly conform because we were not created by God to live in such a sin-filled world in the first place. Thus, when Christ calls us to be different by following and espousing Christian beliefs, principles, and practices, he is summoning us to the lifestyle we were born for.

The most important step in being different for Jesus is realizing and admitting what we really are: We are children of God; we are Christians. Only secondarily are we citizens of a secular world. That world both scorns and disdains us for being different; Jesus both praises and loves us for it.

You gotta get excited to play football, If a guy can't get mad, he doesn't have any business out there.
— *Dicky Lyons Sr.*

The lifestyle Jesus calls us to is different from that of the world, but it is the way we were born to live.

KEEPING THE PEACE

Read Hebrews 12:14-17.

"Make every effort to live in peace with all men and to be holy" (v. 14).

Women with high-heeled shoes" attacked the players; a Kentucky coach slugged the timer. All in all, it was not a night for peace and good will among men or women.

The Fabulous Five of 1953-54 played St. Louis University on Dec. 18 on the road. The game timer used a starter's pistol to signal the end of a half and to call the teams back onto the court after a time out. The timer on this particular night was the son of the St. Louis head coach. In the second half, he let fire right next to UK assistant coach Harry Lancaster, who was sitting at the end of the bench. Lancaster forcefully warned the timer not to do it again.

Soon, however, recalled team member Pete Grigsby, the timer fired the pistol just as close as before, and "the next thing I see is Coach Lancaster grabbing the timer by the collar and punching him so hard he knocked him into the first row of seats." Security officials managed to calm things down.

Until the Cats pulled out to a double-digit lead in the last half on their way to a 71-59 win and the crowd's collective disposition soured. Sophomore Lou Tsioropoulos, who is a member of the UK Athletics Hall of Fame and whose No. 16 jersey has been retired, got into it with the crowd when he fouled out.

That unpleasant repartee upped the level of anger in the gym.

Grigsby said, "Women with high-heeled shoes came down behind our bench and started kicking us in the back and hitting us with their umbrellas." As Grigsby pointed out, the guys on the bench "weren't even playing, and yet we were getting whupped."

After the game, head coach Adolph Rupp told his players not to bother with taking showers but to toss their street clothes into their duffel bags, put their overcoats on over their warmups, and pile into the waiting taxicabs he had called. Grigsby wasn't sure if Rupp were worried about the fans storming the locker room, but the coach was obviously in a hurry to get out of there.

Perhaps you've never been in a brawl or a public brouhaha. But maybe you retaliated when you got one elbow too many in a pickup basketball game. Or maybe you and your spouse or your teenager get into it occasionally, shouting and saying cruel things. Or road rage may be a part of your life.

While we do seem to live in a more belligerent, confrontational society than ever before, fighting is still not the solution to a problem. Rather, it only escalates the whole confrontation, leaving wounded pride, intransigence, and simmering hatred in its wake. Actively seeking and making peace is the way to a solution that lasts and heals broken relationships and aching hearts.

Peacemaking is not as easy as fighting, but it is much more courageous and a lot less painful. It is also exactly what Jesus would do.

I was never so glad for a game to end.
— Pete Grigsby on the '53 game with St. Louis

Making peace instead of fighting takes courage
and strength; it's also what Jesus would do.

DEAD WRONG

Read Matthew 26:14-16; 27:1-10.

"When Judas, who had betrayed him, saw that Jesus was condemned, he was seized with remorse" (v. 27:3).

Many of the experts said this kid coming out of high school named Jodie Meeks couldn't shoot. On one glorious and historic night, he proved them all wrong.

Meeks opted for the pro draft after his junior season of 2008-09. He was First-Team All-SEC and Second-Team All-America that season. He was named to the All-SEC Freshman Team in 2006-07; his sophomore season was shortened to eleven games by an injury. He averaged 23.7 points per game that last season.

For none of that, however, will Meeks be remembered. Instead, he will forever be a part of Wildcat legend and lore for the night of Jan. 13, 2009. That's the evening Meeks "merely rewrote the annals" of college basketball's winningest program.

That night in Knoxville against Tennessee, Meeks scored his first basket 36 seconds into the game, and he never stopped scoring. He had scored 14 of UK's 24 points after 11 1/2 minutes of play and 19 of its first 32 after 14 1/2 minutes. By the first television time out of the last half, Meeks had 36 points.

Still, Tennessee was in the game, trailing by only seven with less than six minutes to play. That's when Meeks iced it, hitting two treys and three foul shots. When the carnage he had wrought was complete and UK had a 90-72 win, Meeks had scored 54 points. That broke Dan Issel's 39-year old UK record of 53. For good measure, Meeks' ten three-pointers were a school record also (breaking the record of nine he shared with Tony Delk).

To provide some perspective, six Division I teams scored fewer points that night than Meeks did. "It was the most unbelievable thing I've ever seen," said head coach Billy Gillispie. The kid who those dead-wrong experts said couldn't shoot scored what was called "a ridiculous" 60 percent of UK's points in the game.

There's wrong, there's dead wrong, and there's Judas wrong. We've all been wrong in our lives, but we can at least honestly ease our conscience somewhat by telling ourselves we'll never be as wrong as Judas was. A close examination of Judas' actions, however, reveals that we can indeed replicate in our own lives the mistake Judas made that drove him to suicidal despair.

Judas ultimately regretted his betrayal of our Lord, but his sorrow and remorse, however boundless, could not save him. His attempt to undo his initial wrong was futile because he tried to fix everything himself rather than turning to God in repentance and begging for mercy.

While we can't literally betray Jesus to his enemies as Judas did, we can match Judas' failure in our own lives by not turning to God in Jesus' name and asking for forgiveness for our sins. In that case, we ultimately will be as dead wrong as Judas was.

Coming out of high school, you'd be surprised at how many people said [Jodie Meeks] couldn't shoot.
— Orestes Meeks on his son

A sin is the first wrong; failing to ask God for forgiveness of it is the second.

TEARS IN HEAVEN

Read Revelation 21:1-8.

*"[God] will wipe every tear from their eyes. There will be
no more death or mourning or crying or pain" (v. 4).*

At Kentucky, Sam Bowie knew that tears are a part of college
basketball.

In 1978, Bowie was the most prized recruit in the country, and
he made the immediate impact everyone expected. He averaged
12.9 points and 8.1 rebounds as a rookie and was All-SEC. The Cats
went 29-6 and were ranked as high as No. 3. Duke nipped them by
one in the NCAA Tournament. As a sophomore, Bowie averaged
17.4 points and 9.1 rebounds and was All-America. The Wildcats
went 22-6 and returned to the Big Dance.

Then the heartbreak and the tears came. Before his junior season,
Bowie broke a leg, an injury that sidelined him for the entire 1981-
82 season. But it got worse. The stress fracture stubbornly refused
to heal and required bone-graft surgery. Bowie missed a second
season. "That was the toughest time," he said, "realizing I would
have to miss another full season."

Bowie was finally healthy for the 1983-84 season, his last in
Lexington. And on March 3, 1984, Senior Night, his tears returned.

Before the game in the locker room, the players joked around,
wondering who would be the first one to shed tears. Bowie was
the last to be introduced and to smash through a hoop with his
face on it. "I couldn't help it," Bowie said. When he broke through

that hoop, he broke down. He was the first.

But more tears came for the emotional senior. With a big lead over LSU that clinched the SEC title, Bowie came out of the game to thunderous applause. He looked to the rafters and thanked the Lord for keeping him healthy that season. Then he hugged Coach Joe B. Hall, went to the bench, and put a towel over his head. "And I just lost it, emotionally, for the second time that night," he said.

When your parents died. When a friend told you that she was divorcing. When you broke your collarbone. When you watch a sad movie.

You cry. Crying is as much a part of life as are breathing and potholes on the highway. Usually pain, sorrow, or disappointment bring on our tears.

But what about when your child was born? When UK wins another NCAA title? When you discovered Jesus Christ? Those times elicit tears too; we cry at the times of our greatest, most overwhelming joy.

Thus, while there will be tears in Heaven, they will only be tears of sheer, unmitigated, undiluted joy. The greatest joy possible, a joy beyond our imagining, must occur when we finally see Christ. If we shed tears when UK wins a game, can we really believe that we will stand dry-eyed and calm in the presence of Jesus?

What we will not shed in Heaven are tears of sorrow and pain.

I was concerned about my teammates seeing me break down, but there was nothing I could do.
— Sam Bowie on the emotion of Senior Night

Tears in Heaven will be like everything else there: a part of the joy we will experience.

THE PIONEER SPIRIT

Read Luke 5:1-11.

*"So they pulled their boats up on shore, left everything
and followed him" (v. 11).*

The pioneer of Kentucky football was a scholar whose only previous experience as a coach was at a girls' school.

Professor A.M. Miller has been called the "daddy" of UK football. A graduate of Princeton, where he apparently developed an enthusiastic interest in the game, he joined the staff of Kentucky State College in 1892. He had previously tried to teach the game to the students at a Pennsylvania girls' school. The school's president had decreed that the girls should learn something about the game so they would not embarrass themselves when they "went down to Princeton or Yale to see the big game."

A group of students persuaded Miller in 1892 to coach the state football team, which played its games in a park that was also used by the school president to pasture his cattle. Miller persuaded him that a grandstand for football should be built on the spot. He then formed a stock company and sold enough shares — primarily to faculty members — to finance the $500 project.

Construction halted when the president ordered that no trees in the park could be removed to make way for the field. That night, though, the offending arbors were chopped down, presumably by a group of students more interested in football than horticulture. The irate president offered a reward for the identity of the culprits, but they were never caught.

The state team lost two straight games, and Miller urged Jackie Thompson, a former Purdue halfback, to take over. Miller became the manager of finances, which meant he had to locate the money for everything but shoes, which the players had to buy themselves.

Thompson was paid solely out of gate receipts. As a faculty member, Miller received no extra money for his work with the team and thus pioneered football at UK solely out of love for the game.

Going to a place in your life you've never been before requires a willingness to take risks and face uncertainty head-on. You may have never helped start a new sports program at a major college, but you've had your moments when your latent pioneer spirit manifested itself. That time you changed careers, volunteered at a homeless shelter, learned Spanish, or went back to school.

While attempting new things invariably begets apprehension, the truth is that when life becomes too comfortable and too familiar, it gets boring. The same is true of God, who is downright dangerous because he calls us to be anything but comfortable as we serve him. He summons us to continuously blaze new trails in our faith life, to follow him no matter what.

Stepping out on faith is risky all right, but the reward is a life of accomplishment, adventure, and joy that cannot be equaled anywhere else.

If I couldn't make it out of gate receipts, I had to foot the deficit.
— UK football pioneer A.M. Miller on being finance manager

**Unsafe and downright dangerous, God calls us
out of the place where we are comfortable to a life
of adventure and trailblazing in his name.**

ATTITUDE CHECK

Read 1 Thessalonians 5:12-22.

*"Give thanks in all circumstances, for this is God's will
for you in Christ Jesus" (v. 18).*

From riding on mail sacks to eating hot dogs, UK's basketball
team of 1943-44 kept on smiling and kept on winning despite pri-
vations and inconveniences brought on by World War II.

Wildcat head coach Adolph Rupp wasn't sure he would be able
to field a team in '43. As he recalled it, "We had only 270 civilians
in school, of whom only three were known to have court experience." Nevertheless, the decision was made in September to have
a team. "The call went out and the boys started rolling out of the
Kentucky hills," Rupp said. He wound up with ten 17-year-olds
too young to enlist and two deferred sophomores.

Lack of experience wasn't the team's only problem that season.
In December, they were to ride by coach to Cincinnati for a game
but got bumped into the baggage car. So how did that discomfort
affect the players' attitude? They "sat around on mail sacks playing
cards and actually seemed to enjoy it more than if they'd been in
Pullmans," Rupp said. They also whipped Cincinnati 58-30.

On a subsequent trip to Champaign, the team had to lay over
to catch a train at 3 a.m. Rupp recalled, "I got the boys to bed early,
awakened them in time, and down we went to the station." When
they arrived, the train hadn't. They learned a derailment down
the line had held the train up. They went back to the hotel for

some more sleep, awoke at 5 to learn the train wouldn't get in before 7, and found out at 7 that the train wouldn't come at all.

So Rupp piled his boys into a bus. The only food they could procure was a bunch of hot dogs from a roadside stand. Surely this affected their attitude. "They sang all the way," Rupp said, "and went out to play the very finest game they've produced all season."

With that kind of attitude, they posted a 19-2 record and were SEC champions.

How's your attitude? You can fuss because your house is not as big as some, because a coworker talks too much, or because you have to take pills every day. Or you can appreciate your home for providing warmth and shelter, the co-worker for the lively conversation, and the medicine for keeping you reasonably healthy.

Whether life is endured or enjoyed depends largely on your attitude. An attitude of thankfulness to God offers you the best chance to get the most out of your life because living in gratitude means you choose joy in your life no matter what your circumstances. This world does not exist to satisfy you, so chances are it will not.

True contentment and joy are found in a deep, abiding relationship with God, and the proper way to approach God is not with haughtiness or anger but with gratitude for all he has given you.

I've had more fun, less grief, and more satisfaction out of coaching this group of youngsters than I ever had before.
— Adolph Rupp on the team of 1943-44

Your attitude goes a long way
toward determining the quality of your life
and of your relationship with God.

DAY 88

ANGER MANAGEMENT

Read James 1:19-27.

"Everyone should be quick to listen, slow to speak and slow to become angry, for man's anger does not bring about the righteous life that God desires" (vv. 19-20).

Derek Anderson was mad, really mad. The result was a big Cat win and one of the most memorable dunks in school history.

Anderson learned his basketball on the playgrounds of Louisville. "I was a U of L fan to the bone," he said, but the Cardinals didn't recruit him. "Are you serious?" he asked himself. "I was just hurt. I felt like I had done everything that was asked of me, and they still didn't want me."

Neither did Kentucky, so Anderson headed to Ohio State in 1992. He scored more than 500 points in Columbus but decided to transfer prior to his junior year when the Buckeyes were hit with NCAA sanctions. UK head coach Rick Pitino didn't repeat the mistake he had made two years before. Anderson sat out a season and then started at guard for the 1995-96 national champs.

Aside from the national title, the highlight of Anderson's UK career came on Dec. 31, 1996, against Louisville, whom he had never forgiven for not recruiting him. His grudge escalated into anger when one of the Cardinals taunted him when they crossed paths in a Louisville mall the day before the game.

"I was mad," he said. "I was mad they didn't recruit me. . . . I was at a boiling point when we started that game." His anger showed in The Dunk. Anthony Epps recovered a loose ball and passed it to Anderson with only one man between him and the basket. A famous photo of the moment shows Anderson almost parallel to the floor "in an absurdly athletic move" as the Cardinal scrambles to get out of the way. Fittingly, Anderson's face was contorted in anger as he screamed.

"I still have a picture of it somewhere in a scrapbook," he said years later. "That was a big, big moment. Hey — I was mad."

He scored 19 points and had six rebounds in the 74-54 win.

Our society today is well aware of anger's destructive power because too many of us don't manage our anger as Derek Anderson did. Anger is a healthy component of a functional human being until — like other normal emotions such as fear, grief, and worry — it escalates out of control. Anger abounds when UK loses; the trouble comes when that anger intensifies from annoyance and disappointment to rage and destructive behavior.

Anger has both practical and spiritual consequences. Its great spiritual danger occurs when anger is "a purely selfish matter and the expression of a merely peevish vexation at unexpected and unwelcome misfortune or frustration." It thus interferes with the living of the righteous, Christ-like life God intends for us.

Our own anger, therefore, can incur God's wrath; making God angry can never be anything but a perfectly horrendous idea.

I always play better when I'm mad.
— *Derek Anderson on playing angry against Louisville*

**Anger becomes a problem when it escalates
into rage and interferes with the righteous life
God intends for us.**

HOME IMPROVEMENT

Read Ephesians 4:7-16.

*"The body of Christ may be built up until we all reach
unity in the faith and in the knowledge of the Son of God
and become mature, attaining to the whole measure of the
fullness of Christ" (vv. 12b, 13).*

From a tiny gymnasium that didn't even have any seats to the
showplace that is Rupp Arena, the Wildcats' home court has
come a long way over the years.

UK's first basketball court was known simply as "The Gymnasium" and was located on the second floor of the north wing of
today's Barker Hall. The court didn't have any seats, so the 650
spectators who could get in had to stand up to watch the games.

To accommodate the overflowing crowds, a man usually stood
outside with a megaphone and relayed to the folks who couldn't
get in what was happening on the court. George Buchheit, UK's
head basketball coach from 1919-24, recalled that "once spectators
got in that old gym we played in there was hardly room to play
the game."

The players also had to dodge the poles that held up the running track that ran around the top of the gym.

The facility was outmoded almost as soon as it was built, and
the public soon called for a better court. In 1924, Alumni Gym with
its "unheard-of" capacity of 2,800 was built for "the outlandish
sum of $92,000." Naysayers immediately derided the building as

WILDCATS

a white elephant that was too big for college basketball.

They were wrong. UK basketball quickly outgrew "the biggest and best gymnasium in the South," leading to Memorial Coliseum, the "House that Rupp Built," in 1950.

One more time, though, the UK program outgrew its home-court until the palace that is 23,000-seat Rupp Arena was opened in 1976. Skeptics again dismissed the building as too big to fill, and once again, they were wrong. Both Kentucky basketball and its facilities just keep getting bigger and better.

You try to improve at whatever you tackle. You attend training sessions and seminars to do your job better. You take golf or tennis lessons and practice to get better. You play that new video game until you master it. To get better at anything requires a dedication involving practice, training, study, and preparation.

Your faith life is no different. Jesus calls us to improve ourselves spiritually by becoming more mature in our faith. We can always know more about God's word, discover more ways to serve God, deepen our prayer life and our trust in God, and do a better job of being Jesus to other people through simple acts of kindness and caring. In other words, we can always become more like Jesus.

One day we will all stand before God as finished products. We certainly want to present him a mature dwelling, a spiritual mansion, not a hovel.

[The Gymnasium] is equipped with the best apparatus that could be procured.
— 1909-11 University Biennial Report

**Spiritual improvement means a constant effort
to become more like Jesus in our day-to-day lives.**

DRY RUN

Read John 4:1-15.

*"Everyone who drinks this water will be thirsty again,
but whoever drinks the water I give him will never thirst.
Indeed, the water I give him will become in him a spring
of water welling up to eternal life" (vv. 13-14).*

One glorious night in January, the Kentucky women ended a drought that had dragged on for twenty frustrating years.

When UK Director of Athletics Mitch Barnhart hired Mickie DeMoss to revive what had become a moribund program, he envisioned just such a night as Jan. 26, 2006. Before the largest crowd ever to watch a women's basketball game at Rupp Arena, the Wildcats knocked off top-ranked Tennessee 66-63. The win was the first for the Wildcats over Tennessee since 1986, a dry run that had stretched across 24 straight losses.

The 15-4 Wildcats played tough all night long, refusing to fold when Tennessee took a five-point lead with 9:38 to play. "We kept our composure," said Jenny Pfeiffer. "A lot of times in the past we would have folded and laid down and let them walk all over us."

A lot of that toughness came from Pfeiffer herself. The junior guard had an interesting odyssey, leaving UK in 2004 after two injury-plagued seasons and enrolling at Louisville before deciding to return to Lexington. She hit all five of her free throws in the last 2:51, including the pair that put UK up 64-63 with 14.8 seconds left. "I was shaking so much," she said about the last trip to the line. "That was probably the biggest pressure situation I've ever been in."

The Lady Vols missed a shot, and junior guard Natassia Alcius got the loose ball and was fouled. With the crowd in an uproar, she hit two foul shots with 2.9 seconds left. Center Sarah Elliott deflected UT's long inbounds pass and then declared the moment to be the greatest in her life. "I think that was the highest I ever jumped," she said about the celebration that began when the horn sounded and officially ended the drought.

The city's put all neighborhoods on water restriction, and as a result, that beautiful lawn you fertilized and seeded is turning a sickly, pale green and may lapse all the way to brown. Somebody wrote "Wash Me" on the rear window of your truck.

The sun bakes everything, including the concrete. The earth itself seems exhausted, just barely hanging on. It's a drought.

It's the way a soul that shuts God out looks.

God instilled the physical sensation of thirst in us to warn us of our body's need for water. He also gave us a spiritual thirst that can be quenched only by his presence in our lives. Without God, we are like tumbleweeds, dried out and windblown, offering the illusion of life where there is only death.

Living water — water of life — is readily available in Jesus. We may drink our fill, and thus we slake our thirst and end our soul's drought — forever.

You're hugging, you're crying, you're screaming, and it's all happening at once. You don't know what to do.
— Sarah Elliott on the end of the drought vs. Tennessee

Our soul thirsts for God's refreshing presence.

TOUGH LOVE

Read Mark 10:17-22.

"'One thing you lack,' [Jesus] said. 'Go, sell everything you have and give to the poor, and you will have treasure in heaven. Then come, follow me.' At this the man's face fell. He went away sad" (vv. 21-22).

An ESPN camera captured UK head coach John Calipari rather forcefully dressing down forward Terrence Jones. That, however, was part of why Jones came to Kentucky in the first place.

Calipari unleashed what was called "an expletive-laced tirade" on his freshman forward during a two-point loss to Alabama on Jan. 18, 2011. But the scene that shocked many and netted Jones a whole bunch of sympathy was just one side of the relationship.

"It's a really good relationship, actually," Jones said in the wake of the publicity generated by Calipari's diatribe, which became national news when the coach publicly apologized on his Twitter account. "He yells at me," Jones admitted, "but you can't be nice all the time or you'll never get anything done." Jones went on to point out the other, rarely seen side of his coach. "He'll say, 'Terrence! I loo-oove you!'" Jones said, pretty fairly mimicking Calipari. "He'll start chasing me and he'll give me a big hug."

In other words, what Calipari gave his young player was tough love — and that's exactly what Jones sought when he decided to play ball for Kentucky. Even his aunt believed Jones needed that kind of relationship. "He's never really been pushed," she said, "and I think that's what he wanted when he chose Kentucky."

Jones flourished under the influence of that tough love. As a freshman in 2010-11, he was the team's second-leading scorer and leading rebounder. He was the SEC Rookie of the Year.

Projected as a first-round draft pick, Jones decided to return to UK for his sophomore season and more of Calipari's tough love. He was the third-leading scorer and rebounder for the national champs and then entered the draft. He was a first-round pick.

Expect your children to abide by your rules? The immediate reward you receive may be an intense and loud "I hate you," a flounce, and a slammed door. So why do you do it? Because you're the parent; you love your children, and you want them to become responsible adults. It's tough love.

Jesus also hands out tough love as the story of the young man illustrates. Jesus broke his heart, but the failure was in the young man, who despite his asseverations of devotion, loved his wealth more than he did Jesus.

Jesus is tough on us, too, in that he expects us to follow him no matter what it costs us. A well-executed flounce won't change anything either. As a parent does for his willful children, Jesus knows what is best for us. We'll appreciate that tough love with all our heart and soul on that glorious day when Jesus welcomes us to the place he has prepared for us.

The sterner the discipline, the greater the devotion.
— Former basketball coach Pete Carril

**Jesus expects us to do what he has told us to do —
but it's because he loves us and wants the best
for us in life and through eternity.**

THE PRIZE

Read Philippians 3:10-16.

"I press on toward the goal to win the prize for which God has called me heavenward in Christ Jesus" (v. 14).

Dan Issel remains rightfully proud that the greatest prize in UK men's basketball — that of all-time leading scorer — remains his. Still, he once tried to talk Rex Chapman into breaking his record.

Issel was so good that more than forty years after he hit his last shot for Kentucky in 1970, he still remains the men's all-time scoring and rebounding leader. (The all-time leading scorer in UK basketball history is Valerie Still with 2,763 points.) Out of high school in 1966, though, Issel wasn't recruited very hard by coach Adolph Rupp. He was the staff's third choice for a center.

During a visit in the spring, Issel saw a recruiting article in the school newspaper, and it "mentioned about 15 guys . . . and my name wasn't mentioned," he recalled. In response to that insult, he dropped Kentucky down on his list of schools. But the other centers being recruiting committed elsewhere, so Rupp put on a late rush and landed him.

In three years of varsity ball (freshmen were ineligible) and without benefit of the three-point shot, the 6-foot-8 All-American center scored 2,138 points. Only Kenny Walker (2,080) and Jack Givens (2,038) have joined Issel in scoring 2,000 points.

Issel has always conceded that the scoring record "is nice," but that winning games was more important to him. The Cats did that; in Issel's three seasons on the varsity UK went 71-12.

Winning is so important to Issel that in 1988 he used breaking his record as a reason to encourage Chapman to stay at UK rather than turning pro. "I told him that if he stayed he would . . . break my record and be the all-time leading scorer at Kentucky, and how neat I thought it was to have that record," Issel said.

His selfless act didn't help; Chapman went to the pros.

Even the most modest and self-effacing among us can't help but be pleased by prizes and honors. They symbolize the approval and appreciation of others, whether it's a school scoring record, an Employee of the Month trophy, a plaque for sales achievement, or recognition for community service.

Such prizes and awards are often the culmination of the pursuit of personal achievement and accomplishment. They represent accolades and recognition from the world. Nothing is inherently wrong with any of that as long as we keep them in perspective.

That is, we must never let awards become such idols that we worship or lower our sight from the greatest prize of all and the only one truly worth winning. It's one that won't rust, collect dust, or leave us wondering why we worked so hard to win it in the first place. The ultimate prize is eternal life, and it's ours through Jesus Christ.

When you look at all of the great players who have played at Kentucky, I'm very proud of that record.
          — Dan Issel on being the men's all-time leading scorer

**God has the greatest prize of all ready
to hand to you through Jesus Christ.**

YOU NEVER KNOW

Read Jonah 1, 2, 3:1-3.

"I, with a song of thanksgiving, will sacrifice to you.
What I have vowed I will make good" (v. 2:9).

You just never know. For instance, a childhood injury that left him unable to raise his left arm was the key to Jack Tingle's becoming a Kentucky basketball legend.

Tingle grew up in the late 1930s shooting at a hoop above the family garage in Bedford, Kent., and he never let the weather keep him from playing basketball. A relative recalled that one winter when she visited the family, she found young Jack had put a hoop up over a door and was shooting basketball in the living room.

An accident when he was 10 changed Tingle's life. He fell from a maple tree and broke his left arm so badly that it never healed correctly. As a result, he could never again raise the arm above his chest. But Tingle used the disability to his advantage; he simply kept shooting and developed a unique right-handed release.

Coach Adolph Rupp signed him in 1943, and Tingle became just one of three Wildcats to earn first-team All-SEC honors four times (1944-47). (The other two are Wallace "Wah Wah" Jones and Ralph Beard.) He was second-team All-America his senior season and was four times named to the All-SEC Tournament team.

He played in an era of the two-handed set shot, but because of his injury, he bewildered defenses with his right-handed release. "He could certainly shoot," said Beard, who played with Tingle on the 1946 team that won the National Invitational Tournament, the equivalent then of the national title.

In 1947, Tingle made more UK history by becoming the first Wildcat player to be drafted by the NBA when the Washington Capitals took him in the first round.

And what made him such a great player resulted in part from the horrible accident that left him with a bum arm.

You never know what you can do until — like Jack Tingle — you want to bad enough or until — like Jonah — you have to because God insists. Serving in the military, maybe even in combat. Standing by a friend while everyone else unjustly excoriates her. Undergoing agonizing medical treatment and managing to smile. You never know what life will demand of you.

It's that way too in your relationship with God. As Jonah the reluctant prophet discovered to his chagrin and his dismay, you never know what God will ask of you. You can know that God expects you to be faithful; thus, you must be willing to trust him even when he calls you to tasks that appear daunting and beyond your abilities.

You can respond faithfully and confidently to whatever God it is calls you to do for him. That's because even though you never know what lies ahead, you can know with absolutely certainty that God will lead you and will provide what you need.

There's one word to describe baseball: You never know.

— *Yogi Berra*

**You never know what God will ask you to do,
but you always know he will provide everything
you need to do it.**

DANCING MACHINE

Read 2 Samuel 6:12-22.

"David danced before the Lord with all his might, while he and the entire house of Israel brought up the ark of the Lord with shouts and the sound of trumpets" (vv. 14-15).

The Kentucky kickoff team found a new way to add excitement to what is perhaps football's most exciting play: They danced.

Commonwealth Stadium was rocking and rolling on Saturday, Oct. 4, 2014, after the Cats connected on a 48-yard touchdown pass to take a 24-17 lead over South Carolina in the third quarter. Then something happened that drove the whole place into a complete frenzy.

The kickoff team routinely trotted onto the field and gathered at the 30-yard line to wait while kicker Austin MacGinnis teed the ball up. A hip-hop song blasted from stadium speakers. The ten players started bouncing to the music's beat, and their movements suddenly morphed into a synchronized dance.

When the sideline and the crowd realized what was happening, they all erupted. "That was the loudest I've ever heard that stadium," said junior cornerback J.D. Harmon, one of the dancers.

Freshman defensive back Kendall Randolph said the players dance "all the time" at practice, usually without music, just to psyche themselves up. Even though he was one of the dancers, he wasn't sure how all ten guys started moving in unison. "Everybody just kind of went at the same time," he said. "I guess it just

WILDCATS

(took off)." However it started, it was spontaneous as the Wildcats insisted the dancing was not choreographed.

Sadly, their first dance was their last dance. The refs made it quite clear that any more dancing on the field would result in an unsportsmanlike conduct penalty. So the Cats didn't dance again — at least not until after the game was over and they had beaten the Gamecocks 45-38. That set off a whole lot of dancing.

One of the more enduring stereotypes of the Christian is of a dour, sour-faced person always on the prowl to sniff out fun and frivolity and shut it down. "Somewhere, sometime, somebody's having fun — and it's got to stop!" Many understand this to be the mandate that governs the Christian life.

But nothing could be further from reality. Ages ago King David, he who would eventually number Jesus Christ among his house and lineage, set the standard for those who love and worship the Lord when he danced in the presence of God with unrestrained joy. Many centuries and one savior later, David's example today reminds us that a life spent in an awareness of God's presence is all about celebrating, rejoicing, and enjoying God's countless gifts, including salvation in Jesus Christ.

Yes, dancing can be vulgar and coarse, but as with David, God looks into our hearts to see what is there. Our very life should be one long song and dance for Jesus.

We didn't plan it. It was just kind of heat-of-the-moment.
— Cornerback J.D. Harmon on the special teams dance

While dancing and music can be vulgar and obscene, they can also be inspiring expressions of abiding love for God.

DANCING MACHINE   189

NOTES
(by Devotion Day Number)

1   that first squad was mostly football . . . in shape during the winter.: Bert Nelli, *The Winning Tradition* (Lexington: The University Press of Kentucky, 1984), p. 13.

1   the Transylvania team showed up for a game with State in 1907 wearing football pads.: Nelli, p. 13.

1   "A good fight was the expected thing.": Nelli, p. 14.

1   Basketball at UK began on . . . and sometimes swept the floor.": Nelli, p. 15.

1   "During the latter part of the game, State College weakened appreciably." Nelli, p. 14.

1   We didn't play for championships but for bloody noses.: Nelli, p. 13.

2   the exhausted runner signaled . . . finish what he had started.: James Streble, "Kentucky Wildcats Football: Jojo Kemp Provides Hero Material," *ASeaofBlue.com*, Oct. 6, 2014, http://www.aseaofblue.com/2014/10/06/6918263/kentucky-wildcats-football-jojo-kemp-provides-hero-material/.

2   When my name was . . . best of my opportunity.: Kyle Tucker, "Jojo Kemp Answers Call for Wildcats," *The Courier-Journal*, Oct. 2, 2014, http://www.courier-journal.com/story/sports/college/kentucky/2014/10/01-jojo-kemp-answers-call-kentucky-football-team/16563825/.

3   declared he had learned it was bad luck to be superstitious.: Russell Rice, *Adolph Rupp* (Champaign, IL: Sagamore Publishing, 1994), p. 21.

3   He always carried a buckeye . . . until the UK fight song had been played.: Nelli, p. 41.

3   In his first season at UK, he spotted . . . The Cats won the game.: Nelli, p. 40.

3   Rupp was careful to step on . . . would feel lucky by game time.: Denny Trease, *Tales from the Kentucky Hardwood* (Champaign, IL: Sports Publishing L.L.C., 2002), p. 71.

3   All forty-two years at UK, . . . and brown socks to every Kentucky game.: Nelli, p. 40.

3   I was thinking if you had those brown socks on.: Nelli, p. 40.

4   My goal is to be the greatest point guard ever.": Grant Wahl, "He's the Shizz," *Sports Illustrated*, Jan. 11, 2010, http://sportsillustrated.cnn.com/vault/article/magazine/MAG1164564/index.htm.

4   break a Fisher-Price rim when they're 3, dunk for real over an opponent at 14,: Wahl, "He's the Shizz."

4   "I did not know his work ethic," . . . He's a killer out there.": Wahl, "He's the Shizz."

4   If I ever accomplish [a goal], I'll set a higher goal and go after that.: Jim & Julie S. Bettinger, *The Book of Bowden* (Nashville: TowleHouse Publishing, 2001), p. 66.

5   "a big Irishman with the features . . . the position of football coach.": Rice, *The Wildcats*, p. 134.

5   he was the team's left halfback . . . ever witnessed a football game.": Rice, *The Wildcats*, p. 135.

5   his rushing average for the day was -2 yards per carry.: Rice, *The Wildcats*, p. 135.

5   he ran into the Centre fullback. . . . simply turn around and tackle you.": Rice, *The Wildcats*, p. 135.

5   I'm inclined to believe he might have been telling the truth.: Rice, *The Wildcats*, p. 135.

6   "As far as I can tell," . . . came down with the rebound.: Curry Kirkpatrick, "Raising the Roof," *Sports Illustrated*, Dec. 14, 1987, http://sportsillustrated.cnn.com/vault/article/magazine/MAG1066835/index.htm.

7   *SI* staff writer William F. Read . . . to name the program's greatest.: William F. Read, "The Alltime Women's Team, *Sports Illustrated*, Oct. 10, 2007, http://sportsillustrated.cnn.com/vault/article/magazine/MAG1115751/index.htm.

7   here is SI's all-time greatest . . . career record for treys made (271).: Read, "The Alltime Women's Team."

7   There's no reason why we can't be one of the premier programs in the nation.: Read, "The Alltime Women's Team."

8   Man, my team's playing scared.": Michael Smith, "Kentucky 70, Florida 55: Showdown Blowdown," *The Courier-Journal*, Feb. 5, 2003, https://secure.pqarchiver.com/courier_journal/access/1832510611.html.

8   He just couldn't look at the . . . "That's it," Smith said.: Michael Smith, "Even Cats Surprised
     They Thrashed Florida, *The Courier-Journal*, Feb. 6, 2003, https://secure.pqarchiver.
     com/courier_journal/access/1832511461.html.

8   "As much as it surprised the spectators, . . . "We were expecting war.": Smith, "Even Cats
     Surprised."

8   Florida's head coach admitted . . . Florida missed 17 of 18 shots.: Smith, "Kentucky 70,
     Florida 55."

8   "I know they said coming to . . . "Tonight was all about having fun.": Smith, "Kentucky 70,
     Florida 55."

9   "a talented athlete with a charismatic personality": "Shipwreck Kelly," *Wikipedia, the free
     encyclopedia*, http://en.wikipedia.org/wiki/Shipwreck_Kelly.

9   "a big, handsome swaggering star": "Shipwreck Kelly," *Wikipedia*.

9   "a flamboyant person with a flair for the spectacular.": Rice, *The Wildcats*, p. 104.

9   on the eve of the 1931 Alabama game, . . . care of Tennessee for you tomorrow.": Rice, *The
     Wildcats*, p. 110.

9   both coaches started their second teams.: Rice, *The Wildcats*, p. 107.

9   Late in the game, the crowd started screaming . . . for a TD on his first play.: Rice, *The Wild-
     cats*, p. 108.

9   In 1959, he was credited with . . . during and after the war.: Rice, *The Wildcats*, p. 111.

10   "SEC West also-rans.": Michael Bradley, *Big Blue* (St Louis: *The Sporting News*, 2002), p. 136.

10   Rick Pitino remained confident at . . . to 11 points with 10 minutes to play.: Trease, p. 142.

10   who hadn't hit a three-pointer in the last eight games,: Trease, p. 142.

10   Kentucky scored the last nine points of the game: Bradley, p. 136.

10   You guys are gonna pay for this tomorrow in practice.; Trease, p. 142.

11   What followed was an unseemly . . . included his ripping off his shirt.: Michael Smith,
     "Wildcats Shoot Down No. 11 Volunteers, 80-78," *The Courier-Journal*, March 2, 2006,
     p. C1, https://secure.pqarchiver.com/courier_journal/access/1771844051.html.

11   Their four misses came on . . . rim as the horn sounded.: Smith, "Wildcats Shoot Down No.
     11 Volunteers."

11   head coach Tubby Smith did . . . "It was crazy in there,": Smith, "Wildcats Shoot Down No.
     11 Volunteers."

12   Joe B. Hall must have had a miraculous vision that day.": Trease, p. 83.

12   Hall revealed his four-part, . . . fans would welcome them home.: Trease, p. 82.

12   everything turned out just exactly . . . They all acted accordingly.: Trease, p. 83.

12   NETS, BUS, POLICE, COLISEUM.: Trease, p. 82.

13   The team "was without question . . . up to that time": Rice, *The Wildcats*, pp. 28-29.

13   Football in Lexington in '97 was still . . . played without helmets or padding.: Rice, *The
     Wildcats*, p. 27.

13   "If ever a team needed help, it was that 1897 crew.": Rice, *The Wildcats*, p. 28.

13   Play was so bad that "rumors persisted that [the team] would be disbanded.": Rice, *The
     Wildcats*, p. 28.

13   Someone had carelessly stored some . . . through a faculty committee.: Rice, *The Wildcats*,
     p. 29.

13   The game I remember most was . . . ran all over the top of us.: Rice, *The Wildcats*, p. 28.

14   Growing up on the mean streets . . . I wanted to continue [my brother's] dream.": Brett Daw-
     son, "After Sibling's Death, Kentucky Basketball's DeAndre Liggins Took Basketball
     Seriously," *The Courier-Journal*, March 31, 2011, https://secure.pqarchiver.com/cou-
     rier_journal/access/2308051291.html.

14   He became a driving force . . . unexpected run to the Final Four.: Dawson, "After Sibling's
     Death."

14   I know my brother looks down . . . I'm just happy about that.: Dawson, "After Sibling's
     Death."

15   "In all the years of Kentucky basketball, . . . the summer before [the] 1969-70 season.": Gregg
     Doyel, *Kentucky Wildcats: Where Have You Gone?* (Champaign, IL: Sports
     Publishing L.L.C., 2005), p. 9.

15   Driving into Lexington for a pickup . . . "There goes the national
     championship.": Doyel, p. 11.

15   Casey's left leg had now deprived him of his explosive first step.: Doyel, p. 11.

15   After UK won the 1996 title, . . . ordered an extra one -- for Casey.: Doyel, p. 13.

16   "I tried to talk him out of coming to Kentucky,": Brett Dawson, "Coach's Brush-Off Lit Fire in Cowgill," *The Courier-Journal*, April 8, 2008, p. C1, https://secure/pqarchiver.com/courier_journal/access/1711005831.html.

16   "I don't know if you're going to be able to play here.": Guy Ramsey, "Where Are They Now: Cowgill," *UKathletics.com*, July 7, 2011, http://www.ukathletics.com/blog/2011/07/where-are-they-now.

16   the new coach on campus . . . better off pursuing other options.: Dawson, "Coach's Brush-Off Lit Fire."

16   "Coach Cohen lit a fire under me," he said. He hit the weight room: Dawson, "Coach's Brush-Off Lit Fire."

16   "He's one of the best outfielders . . . his coach's "lack of recruitment.": Dawson, "Coach's Brush-Off Lit Fire."

16   I dedicated myself to proving [Coach John Cohen] wrong.: Ramsey, "Where Are They Now: Cowgill."

17   "We want to win a title,": John Clay, "Blue Together," *Gr8ness* (Lexington: Lexington Herald-Leader, 2012), p. 120.

17   "We were the best team.": Jerry Tipton, "8th Wonders," *Gr8ness* (Lexington: Lexington Herald-Leader, 2012), p.112.

18   Kentucky head football coach Guy . . . we have to eliminate mistakes,": Chip Cosby, "Wildcats Capitalize on Arkansas Errors," *Lexington Herald-Leader*, Oct. 20, 2002, http://www.kentucky.com/2008/07/08/461727/wildcats-capitalize.

18   "We had too many mistakes,": Cosby, "Wildcats Capitalize."

18   We had made every mistake . . . and were only down by one point.: Cosby, "Wildcats Capitalize."

19   improbable running 10-footer: "Sean Woods," *gofrogs.com*, http://gofrogs.cstv.com/sports/m-baskbl/mtt.woods_sean00.html.

19   During the summer of 1989 . . . I was the only player around.: Trease, p. 129.

19   So the pair headed down to the court. . . . barely made it to that garbage can.": Trease, p. 131.

19   I left the gym that day . . . most grueling preseason camp of our lives.: Trease, p. 131.

20   The Dream Game turned into the Wildest-Dream-Come-True Game for Patrick Sparks.: Pat Forde, "Guard Powers Cats to Win Over Archrival," *Echoes of Kentucky Basketball*, ed. Scott Stricklin (Chicago: Triumph Books, 2006), p. 48.

20   Sparks was the Cats' second-leading . . . "undisputed king of clutch": Forde, "Guard Powers Cats," p. 49.

20   The Cardinals led by ten when . . . to make it a 54-50 game.: Forde, "Guard Powers Cats," p. 49.

20   The pass went into wingman Kelenna . . . and get out of here.": Forde, "Guard Powers Cats," p. 50.

20   "When you think about how it turned out, it's just crazy,": Forde, "Guard Powers Cats," p. 49.

20   It's truly a Cinderella story.: Forde, "Guard Powers Cats, p. 51.

21   As Japanese coach named Mokota . . . for a time in the players' dormitory.: Doyel, p. 54.

21   "I was just reaching out to someone who seemed like he needed a friend,": Doyel, p. 57.

21   Casey gave him rides to practice, ate meals with him,: Doyel, p. 56.

21   helped him understand the terminology and the techniques at practice.: Doyel, pp. 54, 56.

21   He was sitting at home one evening . . . offered Casey a coaching job in Japan.; Doyel, p. 57.

21   "It was a blessing for me,": Doyel, p. 57.

21   They were just small acts of kindness.: Doyel, p. 56.

22   All of a sudden, there was an explosion." . . . in horror at what he saw.: Teddy Greenstein, "Phoenix from Kentucky," *Sports Illustrated*, Oct. 2, 1995, http://sportsillustrated.cnn.com/vault/article/magzine/MAG1007179/index.htm.

22   "I never thought I was doing . . . He has inspired a state.": Luchina Fisher, "Tested by Fire," *People*, Oct. 16, 1995, http://www.people.com/people/archive/article/0,,20101845,00.html.

22   God allowed this to happen . . . maybe change or save a life.: Fisher, "Tested by Fire."

23   In 1968, head coach Adolph . . . answer he never forgot.: Trease, p. 45.

23   "Eighty-six," Starrick said. . . . had not seen a single one of them.: Trease, p. 46.

24   During the time out, he designated Hatton . . . turning any part of his body.: Trease, p. 63.

24   I could see it was dead-on perfect all the way.: Trease, p. 63.

25   Even if the players say . . . 'You've got to win them all,'": Alexander Wolff, "The Untouch-
      ables," *Sports Illustrated*, April 8, 1996, http:sportsillustrated.cnn.com/vault/article/
      magazine/MAG1007945/index.htm.

25   "a masterful, drawn-out trick . . . for my staff and my players,": Wolff, "The Untouchables."

25   "The SEC is too good for us to think of a 16-0 mark.": Wolff, "The Untouchables."

25   "I was glad we lost" . . . the NCAA Tournament.: Wolff, "The Untouchables."

25   He told of meeting the Pope . . . "Oh, you don't have a ring.": Wolff, "The Untouchables."

25   When one preseason publication rated . . . unfolded almost perfectly,: Wolff, "The Untouch-
      ables."

25   Pitino said this team would always . . . never let any of it touch them.": Wolff, "The Un-
      touchables."

25   The only pressure you've got is . . . jump higher and defend better.: Wolff, "The Untouch-
      ables."

26   "State was one of the worst . . . a leg in a previous game.: Rice, *The Wildcats*, p. 36.

26   Convinced that Kentucky University had . . . and from athletic clubs.: Rice, *The Wildcats*,
      pp. 36-37.

26   the team State fielded had only a few students from the school while KU used its own play-
      ers.: Rice, *The Wildcats*, pp. 37-38.

26   Only at the end of the game did the State coach put in his "real" players.: Rice, *The Wildcats*,
      p. 38.

26   In 1904, the chairman of KU's athletic . . . and we will play you.": Rice, *The Wildcats*, p. 39.

26   [Hiring players] has a bad effect on the student body, tending to encourage insubordina-
      tion.: Rice, *The Wildcats*, p. 38.

27   "basketball-mad home, Mason . . . contamination that was Mason County.: Mark Story,
      "The Reason to Stay True Blue," *Gr8ness* (Lexington: Lexington Herald-Leader, 2012),
      p. 18.

27   He also inadvertently "carried . . . his hoops-loving hometown.": Story, p. 18.

27   Miller's success in Lexington . . . Kentucky's earlier snub.: Story, p. 19.

27   You might say time and Darius [Miller] have healed those wounds.: Story, p. 19.

28   He hadn't played in two weeks . . . by the coach not once but twice.: Jerry Tipton, "Fitch
      in Time Saves Bye," *Lexington Herald-Leader*, March 3, 2002, http://www.kentucky.
      com/2008/06/12/532437/fitch-in-time-saves-bye.html.

28   "the player opposing defenses invite . . . capable of making plays,": Tipton, "Fitch in Time
      Saves Bye."

28   who admitted he was surprised . . . when we needed threes,": Tipton, "Fitch in Time Saves
      Bye."

28   I told myself when I came back, I wanted to do something big.: Tipton, "Fitch in Time Saves
      Bye."

29   when Hall met with members of . . . or football coach Guy Morriss. Mark Bechtel, "The
      Music Hall," *Sports Illustrated*, Sept. 17, 2001, http://sportsillustrated.cnn.com/vault/
      article/magazine/MAG1023715/index.htm.

29   "a Renaissance man": "Antonio Hall," *UKAthletics.com*, http://www.ukathletics.com/
      sports/m-footbl/mtt/hall_antonio00.html.

29   He got his musical start . . . so he took up the piano.: Bechtel, "The Music Hall."

29   I could tell right off that [Antonio Hall] was a very special kid.: Bechtel, "The Music Hall."

30   During Issel's junior season of 1968-69, . . . Issel ran.: Ryan Clark, *Game of My Life: Kentucky*
      (Champaign, IL: Sports Publishing L.L.C., 2007), p. 40.

30   "I had to have another 40-point game to break the record,": Clark, p. 38.

30   He didn't know how many points . . . everything was going in,": Clark, pp. 38, 40.

30   As was his practice, reasonably early . . . put Issel back in,": Clark, p. 40.

30   [Coach Rupp] said he was a little sorry . . . wouldn't have put me back in.:
      Clark, p. 40.

31   To a man, said senior All-American . . . He announced his retirement.: Clark, p. 53.

31   "immediately told us this wasn't going to make a difference in the game,": Clark, pp. 53-54.

31   "I've held a grudge against John Wooden all these years. I'll never forget it.": Clark, p. 53.

31   "The first thing I remember about . . . had felt in any other game.": Clark, p. 73.

31   "We never lost that confidence,": Clark, p. 73.

31   "We always felt like we were in control." . . . and finish Duke off.: Clark, p. 74.

31   We felt we were the better team, and we were confident.: Clark, p. 73.

32   Svoboda soon realized "the magnitude . . . and called his dad.: Clark, p. 136.

32   a chemical engineering major and varsity tennis player at Purdue.: Clark, p. 133.

32   he told his son he would regret it . . . had he kept going.: Clark, p. 136.

32   The whole bench jumped off . . .makes it all worthwhile,": Clark, p. 139.

32   Years later he still had an old newspaper . . . still have my piece of net.": Clark, p. 140.

32   It's something I can always tell my kids and my grandkids,": Clark, p. 140.

33   played every minute of all ten games in 1912: Rice, *The Wildcats*, p. 54.

33   On the train rode to Knoxville . . . he had never scored a touchdown,: Rice, *The Wildcats*, pp. 54-55.

33   Joking around, several of Harrison's . . . for the first touchdown.: Rice, *The Wildcats*, p. 55.

33   the ball was given to Harrison: Rice, *The Wildcats*, p. 55.

33   Following a prosperous career . . . making the trip with him.: Rice, *The Wildcats*, p. 55.

33   In 1939, he sent the ball back . . . early days of Kentucky football.: Rice, *The Wildcats*, p. 57.

34   college, not professional baseball, was the . . . more, I felt, than signing.": "Alex Meyer -- From Dream to Team," *The Unbiased MLB Fan*, July 5, 2011, http://nofavoriteteam. mlblogs.com/2011/07/05/alex-meyer.

34   He chose UK because he . . . to come to the games.: "Alex Meyer -- From Dream to Team."

34   "It was the best decision I've made in my life,": Mark Maloney, "Kentucky Baseball's Meyer Commands Attention," *The Lexington Herald-Leader*, May 13, 2011, http://www. kentucky.com/2011/05/13/1739207/kentucky-baseballs-meyer-commands.html.

34   Absolutely, I made the right decision.: Maloney, "Kentucky Baseball's Meyer Commands Attention."

35   Cadets. Colonels. Corn-Crackers. Thoroughbreds.: Rice, *The Wildcats*, p. 49.

35   In chapel the morning after . . . adopted by the football team in 1911.: Rice, *The Wildcats*, p. 49.

35   During a banquet following the 1920 . . . He soon purchased one: Rice, *The Wildcats*, p. 75.

35   that was expressed to Lexington . . . contracted pneumonia and died.: Rice, *The Wildcats*, p. 77.

35   Of battle, [the Wildcat] is not afraid, . . . beasts hold no terror for him.: Rice, *The Wildcats*, p. 49.

36   "Growing up, I always wanted to . . . school needed us, we couldn't leave,": Clark, p. 94.

36   the three may have wished they . . . the 1989-90 Wildcats had only eight players,: Clark, p. 94.

36   "Sometimes, you just have to believe,": Clark, p. 96.

36   Pelphrey used that LSU game to illustrate to his players what can happen if they only believe.: Clark, p. 99.

36   It was all about believing you could do it, and working hard.: Clark, p. 98.

37   the team "undone by egos, bad guard play, and player and coach frustration.": Luke Winn, "Fresh Start," *SI.com*, April 7, 2014, http://www.si.com/vault/2014/04/07/106450916/ fresh-start.

37   It simply took his . . .months to figure it out.: Winn, "Fresh Start."

37   "Hang around in . . . a heart-stopping victory.": Eric Lindsey, "Cats Ride Hollywood Script into National Title Game," *UKathletics.com*, April 5, 2014, http://www.ukathletics.com/ sports/m-baskbl/recaps/040514aaa.html.

37   His hands in the air . . . "Another great game.": Lindsey, "Cats Ride Hollywood Script."

37   This run, these games, . . . a script like this.": Lindsey, "Cats Ride Hollywood Script."

38   He started only one game . . . most dominant basketball team.": Michael Smith, "'Old School' Daniels," *The Courier-Journal*, Feb. 14, 2003, https://secure.pqarchiver.com/ courier_journal/access/1832517071.html.

38   "Erik brings a spark,": Brian Bennett, "Daniels Providing Wildcats a 'Throwback Type of

194

Game,'" *The Courier-Journal*, Dec. 27, 2002, https://secure.pqarchiver.com/courier_journal/access/1834486481.html.

38   "You're talking about a point guard . . . who makes everyone else better.": Smith, "'Old School' Daniels."

38   Tubby Smith agreed with his . . . there on the bench.": Bennett, "Daniels Providing Wildcats a 'Throwback.'"

39   Knight was the kid in the driveway . . . posing for dramatic effect.": Brett Dawson, "Game-Winning Shots Just as Kentucky's Brandon Knight Always Saw Them," *The Courier-Journal*, March 29, 2011, https://secure.pqarchiver.com/courier_journal/access/2305683001.html.

39   I think he just misses on purpose and tries to hit the game-winner.: Brett Dawson, "Brandon Knight: Miss Jumpers, Blow Layups, Sink the Clincher," *The Courier-Journal*, March 26, 2011, https://secure.pqarchiver.com/courier_journal/access/2302109401.html.

40   In the summer of 1994 prior to . . . over the next three weeks, : Trease, p. 147.

40   "the only close game we played all season": Clark, p. 13.

40   "If we had taken five years to . . . Isn't that something?" Nelli, p. 73.

40   Tsioropoulos once said that the team . . . decided to stay home.: Doyel, p. 20.

40   There will be no voting because you guys are not going.: Doyel, p. 20.

41   The team was coached by Dennis' . . . in the country's history.: Sam Farmer, "It's Elementary," *Los Angeles Times*, April 9, 2002, http://www.actuarialoutpost.com/actuarial_discussion_forum/archive/index.php/t-3381.html.

41   Dennis was 5-foot-7 and weighed . . . team until the ninth grade.; Farmer, "It's Elementary."

41   One of the guys on the team had to teach me how to tie my shoes.; Farmer, "It's Elementary."

42   "That was a weird kind of game with all the lead changes,": Brian Bennett, "UK Tops U of L in Overtime," *The Courier-Journal*, Dec. 4, 2003, p. E1, https://secure/pqarchiver.com/courier_journal/access/1816722631.html.

42   After Louisville went up 61-51 . . . to a career-high 18 points.: Bennett, "UK Tops U of L in Overtime."

42   Angela Phillip hit a layup for . . . the basket was waved off,: Bennett, "UK Tops U of L in Overtime."

42   We kept fighting and we didn't give up.: Bennett, "UK Tops U of L in Overtime."

43   Spivey was 6-8 by the time . . . that took up most of the dorm room.": Jennifer Hewlett, "UK All-American Carried Lifelong Scar of '50s Scandal," *Lexington Herald-Leader*, May 9, 1995, http://www.bigbluehistory.net/bb/statistics/Players/Spivey_Bill.html.

43   the coach called him "a mess. . . . with eggs in them.: Trease, p. 41.

43   I'm convinced he can eat, but can he play basketball?: Trease, p. 41.

44   A second game that season ended . . . decided not to play anymore.: Rice, *The Wildcats*, p. 16.

44   A crowd of more than 500 showed up for the game at the Lexington baseball park.: Rice, *The Wildcats*, p. 17.

44   The players wore old gray . . . from their sisters or anybody handy.: Rice, *The Wildcats*, p. 16.

44   The reporter covering the game . . . throughout the Bluegrass area.": Rice, *The Wildcats*, p. 17.

44   In December 1880, a group of students . . . gave him a severe drubbing.": Rice, *The Wildcats*, p. 14.

44   The faculty, who have taken little . . . the athletic feature of the college.: Rice, *The Wildcats*, p. 17.

45   "I just wanted to play . . . to wear the uniform,": Dave Pond, "Blue Blood," *Sharing the Victory Magazine*, March 2011, http://archives.fca.org/vsItemDisplay.1sp?.

45   He called Mills the fattest player he had ever seen: Trease, p. 147.

45   Mills couldn't guard his desk.: Trease, p. 148.

45   "Really, out of desperation, . . . Coach Pitino put me in,": Pond, Blue Blood."

45   During the team practice . . . "greatest shooter in the country" open.: Trease, 150.

45   Nobody saw it coming — least of all me.: Pond, Blue Blood."

46   the game was called after fifteen . . . decided to call it quits.": Rice, *The Wildcats*, p. 30.

| 46 | J.W. Graham said the toughest game . . . after State won the game: Rice, *The Wildcats*, p. 31. |

46   J.W. Graham said the toughest game . . . after State won the game: Rice, *The Wildcats*, p. 31.

46   The faculty committee overseeing athletics . . . after the "Immortals'" season.: Rice, *The Wildcats*, p. 34.

47   Six days prior to the beginning . . . looking better that very afternoon.": Trease, p. 31.

48   "Football was my game," . . . I wanted to eat, sleep, and live it.": Rice, *The Wildcats*, p. 260.

48   Teammate Billy Mitchell, a halfback . . . I ever knew who loved to practice.": Rice, *The Wildcats*, p. 256.

48   he played all but 44 minutes of the 1957 season: Rice, *The Wildcats*, p. 260.

48   a move to middle linebacker for the . . . "Where the football is, you go get it.": Rice, *The Wildcats*, p. 261.

48   On the day we played . . . the greatest player in America.: Rice, *The Wildcats*, p. 256.

49   It was well known that Lyons . . . for his players in Holmes Hall.: Trease: pp. 75-76.

49   He awoke the coach one night . . . every trick he came up with. : Trease, p. 76.

49   A player who lived in Wildcat Lodge . . . little girlfriend crammed inside.; Trease, p. 113.

49   When you run trick plays and . . . folks question your sanity.: Bettinger, p. 32.

50   He quit because the school refused to give him a pay raise.: Rice, *Adolph Rupp*, p. 18.

50   Though he was thinking of . . . to see what UK had to offer.: Rice, *Adolph Rupp*, p. 17.

50   Two university officials met him . . . they also didn't eat so good.": Rice, *Adolph Rupp*, p. 18.

50   Among the athletic council members . . . He was the student representative: Tev Laudeman, "A Freshman Helps Hire UK Coach, Then Plays for Him," *Echoes of Kentucky Basketball*, ed. Scott Stricklin, p. 119.

50   Because he told us he was . . . and convinced us he was.: Rice, *Adolph Rupp*, p. 18.

51   "a 5'10" dynamo" of a guard: Trease, p. 103.

51   "captured the hearts of the fans.": Trease, p. 103.

51   Early in the season, though, Beal's effectiveness . . . said it was worth a try.: Trease, p. 104.

51   Hall found him on the training table, . . . he started moving better.": Trease, p. 104.

52   "was one of those natural worriers . . . hung over his head.": Rice, *The Wildcats*, p. 94.

52   the university didn't offer scholarships . . . a job with a downtown business.: Rice, *The Wildcats*, p. 97.

52   "We worked two or three hours . . . a clean bed to sleep in,": Rice, *The Wildcats*, p. 98.

52   Gamage was described as "debonair" . . . the actual dire situation.": Rice, The Wildcats, p. 94.

53   "an impossible dream come true,": Pat Forde, "It's Moss' Big Dream Come True; Tubby's, Too," *The Courier-Journal*, Jan. 4, 2004, p. C1, https://secure/pqarchiver.com/courier_journal/access/1813328711.html.

53   the guy who got a standing . . . the wildly enthusastic applause: Forde, "It's Moss' Big Dream."

53   nothing about the game brought . . . envisioning himself wearing UK Blue.: Forde, "It's Moss' Big Dream."

54   Allen had to battle for playing time: Vaught, p. 124.

54   In the first half of the Auburn . . . I haven't been in the game.": Vaught, p. 124.

54   He didn't even slow down when he . . . hasn't done anything to help us.: Vaught, p. 125.

54   Maybe if you put me in, I could help you.: Vaught, p. 125.

55   We're in a street fight. . . . to see who has my back.": Chip Cosby, "Operation Wow!" *Lexington Herald-Leader*, Oct. 17, 2010, http://www.kentucky.com/2010/10/17/1482854/operation-wow.-kentucky-stuns-no.html.

55   "it was time for them to put up their dukes": Cosby, "Operation Wow!"

55   "All our defense did is come out . . . thought we were going to lose that game.": Cosby, "Operation Wow!"

55   We came with 80 guys, and all 80 of them had my back.: Cosby, "Operation Wow!"

56   he was so ignored by the media . . . and had a lot of energy,": Jerry Tipton, "Estill Steals Center Stage," *Lexington Herald-Leader*, March 18, 2001, http://www.kentucky.com/2008/06/12/532407/estill-steals-center-stage.html.

56   The sub of a sub was . . . 11 points and grabbed five rebounds.: Tipton, "Estill Steals Center Stage."

56   "The rims are nice out there,": Tipton, "Estill Steals Center Stage."

56   They probably didn't know too much about me. A lot of teams don't.: Tipton, "Estill Steals

196

Center Stage."

57 Rupp taught him to get up first, . . . other guy's shoulder for leverage: Rice, *Adolph Rupp*, p. 177.

57 Riley lost only twelve of fifty-eight jumps: Rice, *Adolph Rupp*, p. 175.

57 once beat a seven-footer to the ball: Rice, *Adolph Rupp*, p. 177.

57 "that people didn't have a whole lot . . . wouldn't be one of the contenders.: Nelli, p. 83.

57 the Runts were "one of the finest . . . they were very quick.": Nelli, p. 83.

57 They averaged 6-foot-3.: Nelli, p. 84.

57 Rupp would "close his eyes and listen . . . the ball being passed to perfection.": Rice, *Adolph Rupp*, p. 175.

58 "dawn-to-dusk toil in the fields . . . battle for survival on the prairie.": Nelli, p. 36.

58 While the older boys worked the fields, . . . wild horses for some extra money.: Rice, *Adolph Rupp*, p. 4.

58 He worked as the school janitor, . . . all for fifty cents a month.": Rice, *Adolph Rupp*, p. 5.

58 So they could go to school . . . sleeping outdoors on straw.: Rice, *Adolph Rupp*, p. 6.

58 It was hard work from sunup until sundown. I enjoyed that.: Ripe, *Adolph Rupp*, p. 6.

59 halfback Jake Gaiser . . . exploded during the mad scramble.: Rice, *The Wildcats*, p. 50.

59 J. White Guyn earned a fifth . . . but nothing came of it.": Rice, *The Wildcats*, p. 39.

59 "Kentucky's most important victory . . . asked for a longer game,: Rice, *The Wildcats*, p. 47.

59 He told them that his players . . . Illinois didn't ask for an extension: Rice, *The Wildcats*, p. 48

59 I'm not too proud to change. I like to win too much.: Bettinger, p. 15.

60 Freshman guard Dwight Anderson scored . . . nailed a 15-foot jumper: Trease, p. 99.

60 A Kansas player signalled for a timout -- but the Hawks had used them all.: Trease, p. 99.

60 "I would line up my toe right in . . . sight the basket and let it go.": Trease, p. 100.

60 I had to use some body English and almost walk it in.: Trease, p. 100.

61 "I couldn't believe it," he recalled. "I was just in shock.": Clark, p. 192.

61 "For Kentucky kids who saw Duke beat Kentucky in 1992, [the game] did mean more to us,": Clark, p. 193.

61 Padgett set a screen for star . . . yelling and screaming, "We got this!": Clark, p. 195.

61 Coach Tubby Smith elected to guard . . . fell into Padgett's arms.: Clark, p. 195.

61 "I should own that [game] ball . . . 18 points and 11 rebounds, grabbed it.: Clark, p. 195.

61 It was a victory that provided payback.: Clark, p. 196.

62 Many experts considered the Warriors . . . some onto the window sills." Neville Dunn, "Sensational Long Shot by Red Hagan Gives Kentucky 35 to 33 Triumph," *Lexington Herald*, Feb. 14, 1938, http://www.bigbluehistory.net/bb/Statistics/Games/19380214Marquette.html.

62 As the Cats prepared to inbounds . . . and then blessed himself again.: Dunn, "Sensational Long Shot."

62 "A voice said to me," . . . the ball caromed off the backboard: Dunn, "Sensational Long Shot."

62 Exuberant fans stormed onto the floor . . . his prayer-guided shot.: Dunn, "Sensational Long Shot."

62 I shot and it went through.: Dunn, "Sensational Long Shot."

63 " a team that had . . . shy of the national title.": Jeff Eisenberg, "John Calipari Reveals the Famous 'Tweak," *The Dagger*, April 14, 2014, http://www.sports.yahoo.com/blogs/ncaab-the-dagger/john-calipari-reveals-the-famous--tweak--that-sparked-kentucky-s-march-revival-152646207.html.

63 Right before the SEC . . . has since been debated.: Eisenberg, "John Calipari Reveals."

63 I messed this up. Make me look good now.: Eisenberg, "John Calipari Reveals."

64 "I shouldn't have done this," . . . before the Senior Night celebration: Michael Smith, "Kentucky 106, Vanderbilt 44," *The Courier-Journal*, March 6, 2003, p. E1, https://secure.pqarchiver.com/courier_journal/access/1832531251.html.

64 "lump-in-your-throat . . . this Senior Night from the others.": Smith, "Kentucky 106, Vanderbilt 44."

64 "As badly as John wanted to play . . . I've been a part of,": Smith, "Kentucky 106, Vanderbilt 44."

64 It took a lot of courage for John and Feleica [Stewart] to do this.: Smith, "Kentucky 106, Vanderbilt 44."

65 There was the welcome party . . . Fellowship of Christian Athletes breakfast.: Brett Dawson, "Mixing Bowl: UK Balances Fun, Work," *The Courier-Journal*, Dec. 27, 2006, p. C1, https://secure.pqarchiver.com/courier_journal/access/1749405051.html.

65 On Dec. 26, at their first practice . . . turn it on and turn it off,": Dawson, "Mixing Bowl."

65 We've got to have fun . . . when it's time for football.: Dawson, "Mixing Bowl."

66 "In college I discovered I liked . . . rude awakening, I would say,": Doyel, p. 151.

66 His true with Rupp was an unsteady . . . because of his YMCA competition.: Doyel, p. 153.

66 The Boston Celtics drafted him . . . when they drafted him in '61.: Doyel, p. 153.

66 I think I have maybe a different perspective than most people.: Doyel, p. 153.

67 "We'll celebrate later.": Glen Rosales, "No Easy Task for Kentucky Women to Sink Hampton," *The Courier-Journal*, March 18, 2011, https://secure.pqarchiver.com/courier_journal/access/2297572321.html.

67 at a news conference before . . . "We'll celebrate later.": Rosales, "No Easy Task for Kentucky Women."

68 "big and tough and strong: Nelli, p. 22.

68 He would just slam into guys." . . . and very rarely shot the ball.: Nelli, p. 23.

68 the Washington and Lee basketball team showed . . . turned out for the game.: Norris Royden, "Wildcats Come from Behind in Second Half to Beat Washington-Lee, 44-34," *Lexington Herald*, Feb. 5, 1926, http://www.bigbluehistory.net.bb/Statistics/Games/19260205WashingtonLee.html.

69 Jones decided to give up football . . . and refused to play him.: Trease, p. 53.

69 On the road, Rupp would retire . . . to socialize and talk basketball.: Trease, pp. 53, 55.

69 After Temple beat the Cats 60-59, . . . the rest of the season,: Trease, p. 55.

70 "the punt was football's most important and efficient weapon.": Rice, *The Wildcats*, p. 121.

70 with UK leading in the closing . . . kicked out of a stadium,": Rice, *The Wildcats*, p. 114.

70 "The mud was knee deep that day," . . . they couldn't do anything with it.: Rice, *The Wildcats*, p. 122.

70 The Cats didn't run a play from . . . only 22 the entire game to W&L's 24.: Rice, *The Wildcats*, p. 124.

70 Seventy times that grimy, slippery football sailed into the air.: Rice, *The Wildcats*, p. 121.

71 Prior to the Battle for . . . physical to the extreme.": Pat Forde, "Kentucky's Kidd-Gilchrist Comes of Age in Slugfest," *Yahoo!Sports*, Dec. 31, 2011, http://rivals.yahoo.com/ncaa/basketball/news?slug=pf-forde_kidd_gilchrist_kentucky_louisville.

71 The boss Cat knew . . . forearms and shrieking whistles.": John Clay, "Kidd-Gilchrist Proves Mettle on Big State," *Gr8ness* (Lexington: Lexington Herald-Leader, 2012), p. 30.

71 "He wasn't bothered . . . by the physical play,": Clay, "Kidd-Gilchrist Proves Mettle."

71 He had to overcome . . . letter-of-intent to UK.: Forde, "Kentucky's Kidd-Gilchrist."

71 Kidd-Gilchrist admitted he . . . to win the game,": Forde, "Kentucky's Kidd-Gilchrist."

71 I'm built for this. I just love the challenge.: Forde, "Kentucky's Kidd-Gilchrist."

72 While admitting the win was one . . . beat any team in the nation,": Chip Cosby, "No Miracles Necessary," *Lexington Herald-Leader*, Oct. 14, 2007, http://www.kentucky.com/2008/07/07/454738/no-miracles-necessary-as-cats.html.

72 "I can't say enough about . . . guts of this football team,": Cosby, "No Miracles Necessary."

72 Woodson let fly just before he was drilled,: Cosby, "No Miracles Necessary."

72 It's got to be right up there at the top.: Cosby, "No Miracles Necessary."

73 Delk later admitted that playing . . . on guard Travis Ford for help.: Vaught, pp. 175-76.

73 the "dreaded" point guard.: Vaught, p. 177.

73 Pitino said the position change . . . moving Delk back to point guard.: Vaught, p. 178.

73 Pitino later admitted that had he . . . UK probably wouldn't have won the title.: Vaught, p. 178.

74 he called Rondo into his . . . made me feel good.": Michael Smith, "Rondo Earns His Stripes," *The Courier-Journal*, Dec. 18, 2005, p. C1, https://secure.pqarchiver.com/courier_journal/access/1775151611.html.

74 "He was like a captain out there, . . . He's the guy who got us going,": Smith, "Rondo Earns His Stripes."

WILDCATS

74   "ambivalent, vacillating, impulsive, unsubmissive.": MacArthur, p. 39.

74   "the greatest preacher among . . . figure" in the birth of the church.: MacArthur, p. 39.

75   "a virtual iron man," . . . about playing without tape,": Rice, *The Wildcats*, p. 84.

75   Sanders also required special equipment . . . barely move his arms at all.: Rice, *The Wildcats*, p. 86.

75   Sandy, if you had any brains, you'd quit.: Rice, *The Wildcats*, p, 84.

76   UK's defensive specialist, Tom Kron, . . . to take the shot.: Trease, p. 59.

76   "hadn't done much" -- banked in a 13-foot shot: Clark, p. 28.

76   The next morning, the headline . . . to Take the Winning Shot.": Clark, p. 29.

76   He set up a play for Nash . . . defense really kept me covered.": Clark, p. 28.

76   "I really had no choice but . . . you to take the last shot.": Trease, p. 60.

76   [Tommy] Mobley may have been . . . to take the vital shot.: Clark, p. 29.

77   The list and the quote pertaining to Jamal Mashburn are from an article by Dan Bodner, "Kentucky Basketball: The 25 Best Players in the Program's Long History," *bleacherreport.com*, Jan. 27, 2011, http://bleacherreport.com/articles/582612-kentucky-basketball.

78   The team went straight to the . . . during a two-hour practice.: Rice, *The Wildcats*, p. 216.

78   Bryant simply kept moving his team . . . several times to enjoy the scenery.: Rice, *The Wildcats*, p. 217.

78   "Boys, hold your heads up. It's my fault. I just worked you too hard.": Rice, *The Wildcats*, p. 218.

78   Bryant put his team through . . . in pads in the afternoon.: Rice, *The Wildcats*, p. 218.

78   Bryant told us he had learned something at Cocoa.: Rice, *The Wildcats*, p. 218.

79   a fixture in the UK athletics department . . . started shooting as a teenager: "Harry Mullins: Profile," *UKathletics.com*, http://www.ukathletics.com/sports/c-rifle/mtt/mullins_harry00.html.

79   That amounted to a fraction of an inch . . . "And that's over 480 shots.": Chris White, "Kentucky Rifle Tam Holds Off West Virginia to Win First NCAA Championship, *KentuckySports.com*, March 13, 2011, http://www.kentucky.com/2011/03/13/1668702/kentucky-rifle-team-holds-off.html.

80   Bob Brannum was the youngest . . . was too young for the draft: Doyel, p. 27.

80   After he turned 18 in May, . . . couldn't crack the lineup as a starter.: Doyel, p. 29.

80   Jim Jordan had twice been . . . trouble getting playing time.: Roy Steinfort, "Rupp Chose Freshmen Over 2 Ex-All-Americans," *Louisville Courier-Journal*, Feb. 28, 1947, http://www.bigbluehistory.net.bb/dateline.html#allamericans.

80   Two freshmen, Jim Line and . . . those voting against the idea.: Steinfort, "Rupp Chose Freshmen."

80   There wasn't much Rupp could do. He only had ten players.: Steinfort, "Rupp Chose Freshmen."

81   "as if the Bulldogs had been in the Wildcats' huddle during the timeout.": Michael Smith, "'Somebody Loves Us Up There,'" *The Courier-Journal*, Jan. 15, 2004, p. E1, https://secure.pqarchiver.com/courier_journal/access/1813332741.html.

81   Guard Gerald Fitch, whose hot . . . as there's ever been.": Smith, "'Somebody Loves Us Up There.'"

81   "We were a little lucky tonight,": Pat Forde, "The Fluke Preserves The Streak for Cats," *The Courier-Journal*, Jan. 14, 2004, p. E1, https://secure.pqarchiver.com/courier_journal/access/1813327421.html.

81   I'd rather be lucky than good, but I think we have a combination of both.": Forde, "The Fluke."

82   Lyons "was known to commit . . . one guy who is messin' up,": Myron Cope, "Dicky Does a Bit of Everything But Dicker," *Sports Illustrated*, Nov. 11, 1968, http://sportsillustrated.cnn.com/vault/article/magazine/MAG1081797/index.htm.

82   In the '67 Vandy game, . . . and Lyons scored.: Rice, *The Wildcats*, p. 303.

82   Word had it that Lyons led . . . an inveterate player of the horses.: Cope, "Dicky Does a Bit of Everything."

82   You gotta get excited . . . have any business out there.: Cope, "Dicky Does a Bit of Everything."

83   Women with high-heeled shoes": Trease, p. 23.

83 The game timer used a starter's pistol . . . the St. Louis head coach.: Trease, p. 22.

83 In the second half, he let fire . . . storming the locker room,: Trease, p. 23.

83 I was never so glad for a game to end.: Trease, p. 23.

84 Many of the experts said . . . Jodie Meeks couldn't shoot.: Pat Forde, "Meeks Puts on a Show for the Ages," *ESPN*, Jan. 13, 2009, http://sports.espn.go.com/espn.columns/ story?columnist=forde_pat&id=3831403.

84 "merely rewrote the annals" of college . . . Meeks had 36 points.: Forde, "Meeks Puts on a Show."

84 That's when Meeks iced it, hitting two treys and three foul shots.: Forde, "Meeks Puts on a Show."

84 six Division I teams scored . . . "a ridiculous" 60 percent: Forde, "Meeks Puts on a Show."

84 Coming out of high school, you'd . . . [Jodie Meeks] couldn't shoot.: Forde, "Meeks Puts on a Show."

85 Sam Bowie was the most prized recruit in the country.: Clark, p. 77.

85 "That was the toughest time," he said, "realizing I would have to miss another full season.": Clark, p. 78.

85 Before the game in the locker room, . . . He was the first.: Clark, p. 81.

85 Bowie came out of the game . . . for the second time that night,": Clark, p. 82.

85 I was concerned about my teammates seeing me break down, but there was nothing I could do.: Clark, p. 81.

86 Professor A.M. Miller has been called . . . should be built on the spot.: Rice, *The Wildcats*, p. 18.

86 He then formed a stock company . . . to finance the $500 project.: Rice, *The Wildcats*, pp. 18, 20.

86 Constructed halted when the president . . . in football than horticulture.: Rice, *The Wildcats*, p. 20.

86 The irate president offered a reward. . . , but they were never caught.: Rice, *The Wildcats*, pp. 20-21.

86 Miller urged Jackie Thompson, . . . for his work with the team: Rice, *The Wildcats*, p. 21.

86 If I couldn't make it out of gate receipts, I had to foot the deficit.: Rice, *The Wildcats*, p. 21.

87 "We had only 270 civilians . . . and two deferred sophomores.: Arthur Daley, "His Old Kentucky Home," *Echoes of Kentucky Basketball*, ed. Scott Stricklin, p. 125.

87 In December, they were to ride . . . if they'd been in Pullmans," Daley, "His Old Kentucky Home," p. 125.

87 On a subsequent trip to . . . they've produced all season.": Daley, "His Old Kentucky Home, p. 125.

87 I've had more fun, less grief . . . than I ever had before.: Daley, "His Old Kentucky Homes," p. 125.

88 "I was a U of L fan to the bone," . . . they still didn't want me.": Clark, p. 165.

88 His grudge escalated into anger . . . the day before the game.: Clark, p. 168.

88 "I was mad," he said. . . . when we started that game.: Clark, p. 169.

88 Anthony Epps recovered a loose ball . . . between him and the basket.; Clark, p. 169.

88 A famous photo of the moment shows . . . Hey -- I was mad.": Clark, p. 170.

88 I always play better when I'm mad.: Clark, p. 168.

89 UK's first basketball court was known . . . too big for college basketball.: Nelli, p. 6.

89 "the biggest and best gymnasium in the South,": Nelli, p. 8.

89 skeptics agains dismissed the building as too big to fill,: Nelli, p. 8.

89 [The Gymnasium] is equipped with the best apparatus that could be procured.: Nelli, p. 6.

90 When UK Director of Athletics Mitch . . . he envisioned just such a night: Brian Bennett, "UK Knocks Off Lady Vols 66-63," *The Courier-Journal*, Jan. 27, 2006, p. C1, https:// secure.pqarchiver.com/courier_journal/access/1771834491.html.

90 "We kept our composure," . . . let them walk all over us.": Bennett, "UK Knocks Off Lady Vols."

90 She hit all five of her free . . . the highest I ever jumped,": Bennett, "UK Knocks Off Lady Vols."

90 You're hugging, you're crying, . . . You don't know what to do.: Bennett, "UK Knocks Off Lady Vols."

91   An ESPN camera captured . . . down forward Terrence Jones.: Brett Dawson, "Tough Love," *The Courier-Journal*, Jan. 28, 2011, p. C1, https://secure.pqarchiver.com/courier_journal/access/2251846991.html.

91   Calapari unleashed what was called "an expletive-laced tirade: Dawson, "Tough Love."

91   "It's a really good relationship, . . . he'll give me a big hug.": Dawson, "Tough Love."

91   "He's never really been pushed," . . . when he chose Kentucky.": Dawson, "Tough Love."

92   He was the staff's third choice for a center.: Vaught, p. 10.

92   During a vist in the spring, . . . Rupp put on a late rush.: Vaught, p. 11.

92   the scoring record "is . . . was more important to him.: Vaught, p. 9.

92   "I told him that if . . . was to have that record.": Vaught, p. 10.

92   When you look at all . . . I'm very proud of that record.: Vaught, p. 9.

93   shooting at a hoop above the family . . . a unique right-handed release.: Ben Fronczek, "Bedford's Jack Tingle Reached Basketball's Pinnacle in the 1940s," *RoundAbout*, March 2001, http://www.roundaboutmadison.com/Inside%20Pages/Archived%20Article/2001/3.

93   He played in an era of . . . "He could certainly shoot,": Fronczek, "Bedford's Jack Tingle Reached Basketball's Pinnacle."

94   The ten players started bouncing . . . was not choreographed.: Kyle Tucker, "UK's Kickoff Team Savors Its Last Dance," *The Courier-Journal*, Oct. 9, 2014, http://www.courier-journal.com/story/sports/college/kentucky/2014/10/09/kentucky-footballs-kickoff-team-savors-last-dance/16981141/.

94   The refs made it quite . . . unsportsmanlike conduct penalty.: Tucker, "UK's Kickoff Team Savors Its Last Dance."

94   We didn't plan it. It was just kind of heat-of-the-moment.: Tucker, "UK's Kickoff Team Savors Its Last Dance."

KENTUCKY

BIBLIOGRAPHY

"Alex Meyer -- From Dream to Team." *The Unbiased MLB Fan.* http://nofavoriteteam.ml-blogs.com/2011/07/05/alex-meyer-from-dream-to-team/html.

"Antonio Hall." *UKathletics.com.* http://www.ukathletics.com/sports/m-footbl/mtt/hall_antonio00.html.

Bechtel, Mark. "The Music Hall." *Sports Illustrated.* 17 Sept. 2001. http://sportsillustrated.cnn.com/vault/article/magazine/MAG1023715/index.htm.

Bennett, Brian. "Daniels Providing Wildcats a 'Throwback Type of Game.'" *The Courier-Journal.* 27 Dec. 2002. https://secure/pqarchiver.com/courier_journal/access/1834486481.html.

---. "UK Knocks Off Lady Vols 66-63." *The Courier-Journal.* 27 Jan. 2006. C1. https://secure/pq archiver.com/courier_journal/access/1771834491.html.

---. "UK Tops U of L in Overtime." *The Courier-Journal.* 4 Dec. 2003. E1. https://secure/pqarchiver.com/courier_journal/access/1816722631.html.

Bettinger, Jim & Julie S. *The Book of Bowden.* Nashville: TowleHouse Publishing, 2001.

Bodner, Dan. "Kentucky Basketball: The 25 Best Players in the Program's Long History." *bleacherreport.com.* 27 Jan. 2011. http://bleacherreport.com/articles/582612-kentucky-basketball.

Bradley, Michael. *Big Blue: 100 Years of Kentucky Wildcats Basketball.* St. Louis: *The Sporting News.* 2002.

Clark, Ryan. *Game of My Life: Kentucky: Memorable Stories of Wildcat Basketball.* Champaign, IL: Sports Publishing L.L.C., 2007.

Clay, John. "Blue Together: Kentucky Does It Right by Doing It Together." *Gr8ness: Celebrating the Kentucky Wildcats' 8th National Championship.* Lexington: Lexington Herald-Leader, 2012. 120-21.

-----. "Kidd-Gilchrist Proves Mettle on Big Stage." *Gr8ness: Cele-brating the Kentucky Wildcats' 8th National Championship.* Lexington: Lexington Herald-Leader, 2012. 30-31.

Cope, Myron. "Dicky Does a Bit of Everything But Dicker." *Sports Illustrated.* 11 Nov. 1968. http://sportsillustrated.cnn.com/vault/article/magazine/MAG1081797/index.htm.

Cosby, Chip. "No Miracles Necessary as Cats Beat No. 1, Solidify Status." *Lexington Herald-Leader.* 14 Oct. 2007. http://www.kentucky.com/2008/07/07/454738/no-miracles-necessary-as-cats.html.

---. "Operation Wow! Kentucky Stuns No. 10 South Carolina." *Lexington Herald-Leader.* 17 Oct. 2010. http://www.kentucky.com/2010/10/17/1482854/operation-wow.-kentucky-stuns-no.html.

---. "Wildcats Capitalize on Arkansas Errors, Win 29-17." *Lexington Herald-Leader.* 20 Oct. 2002. http://www.kentucky.com/2008/07/08/461727/wildcats-capitalize.

Daley, Arthur. "His Old Kentucky Home." *Echoes of Kentucky Basketball: The Greatest Stories Ever Told.* Ed. Scott Stricklin. Chicago: Triumph Books, 2006. 124-26.

Dawson, Brett. "After Sibling's Death, Kentucky Basketball's DeAndre Liggins Took Basketball Seriously." *The Courier-Journal.* 31 March 2011. https://secure.pqarhiver.com/courier_journal/access/2308051291.html.

---. "Brandon Knight: Miss Jumpers, Blow Layup, Sink the Clincher — Then Repeat." *The Courier-Journal.* 26 March 2011. https://secure.pqarchiver.com/courier_journal/access/2303109401.html.

---. "Coach's Brush-Off Lit fire in Cowgill." *The Courier-Journal.* 8 April 2008. C1. https://secure.pqarchiver.com/courier_journal/access/1711005831.html.

---. "Game-Winning Shots Just as Kentucky's Brandon Knight Always Saw Them." *The Courier-Journal.* 29 March 2011. https://secure.pqarchiver.com/courier_journal/access/2305683001.html.

---. "Mixing Bowl: UK Balances Fun, Work." *The Courier-Journal.* 27 Dec. 2006. C1. https://

secure/pqarchiver.com/courier_journal/access/1749405051.html.

---. "Tough Love: Aunt Says Calapari Is Giving Jones a Needed Push." *The Courier-Journal.* 28 Jan. 2011. C1. https://secure.pqarchiver.com/courier_journal/access/2251846991. html.

Doyel, Gregg. *Kentucky Wildcats: Where Have You Gone?* Champaign, IL: Sports Publishing L.L.C., 2005.

Dunn, Neville. "Sensational Long Shot by Red Hagan Gives Kentucky 35 to 33 Triumph over Marquette Five." *Lexington Herald.* 14 Feb. 1938. http://www.bigbluehistory.net/bb/Statistics/Games/19380214Marquette.html.

Eisenberg, Jeff. "John Calipari Reveals the Famous 'Tweak' That Sparked Kentucky's March Revival." *The Dagger.* 14 April 2014. http://www.sports.yahoo.com/blogs/ncaab-the-dagger/john-calipari-reveals-the-famous--tweak--that-sparked-Kentucky-s-march-revival-152646207.html.

Farmer, Sam. "It's Elementary: NFL Prospect Dennis Johnson Began His Career as a High School Player at Age 6." *Los Angeles Times.* 9 April 2001. http://www.actuarialoutpost.com/actuarial_discussion_forum/archive/index.php/t-3381.html.

Fisher, Luchina. "Tested by Fire." *People.* 16 Oct. 1995. http://www.people.com/people/archive/article/0,,20101845,00.html.

Forde, Pat. "Guard Powers Cats to Win Over Archrival." *Echoes of Kentucky Basketball: The Greatest Stories Ever Told.* Ed. Scott Stricklin. Chicago: Triumph Books, 2006. 48-51.

---. "It's Moss' Big Dream Come True; Tubby's, Too." *The Courier-Journal.* 4 Jan. 2004. C1. https://secure.pqarchiver.com/courier_journal/access/1813328711.html.

-----. "Kentucky's Kidd-Gilchrist Comes of Age in Slugfest." *Yahoo!Sports.* 31 Dec. 2011. http://www.rivals.yahoo.com/ncaa/basketball/news?slug=pf-forde_kidd_gilchrist_kentucky_louisville.

---. "Meeks Puts on a Show for the Ages." *ESPN.* 13 Jan. 2009. http://sports.espn.co.com/espn/column/story?columnist=forde_pat&id=3831403.

---. "The Fluke Preserves The Streak for Cats." *The Courier-Journal.* 14 Jan. 2004. E1. https://secure/pqarchiver.com/courier_journal/access/1813327421.html.

Fronczek, Ben. "Bedford's Jack Tingle Reached Basketball's Pinnacle in the 1940s." *Round-About.* March 2001. http://www.roundaboutmadison.com/Inside%20Pages/Archived%20Articles/2001/3.

Greenstein, Teddy. "Phoenix from Kentucky." *Sports Illustrated.* 2 Oct. 1995. http://sportsillustrated.cnn.com/vault/article/magazine/MAG1007179/index.htm.

"Harry Mullins: Profile." *UKathletics.com.* http://www.ukathletics.com/sports/c-rifle/mtt/mullins_harry00.html.

Hewlett, Jennifer. "UK All-American Carried Lifelong Scar of '50s Scandal." *Lexington Herald-Leader.* 9 May 1995. http://www.bigbluehistory.net/bb/statistics/Players/Spivey_Bill.html.

Howlett, Ken. "Q&A with Former Wildcat Cameron Mills." *aseaofblue.com.* 11 March 2010. http://www.aseaofblue.com/2010/3/11/1367040/q-a-with-former-wildcat-cameron-mills.

Kirkpatrick, Curry. "Raising the Roof." *Sports Illustrated.* 14 Dec. 1987. http://sportsillustrated.cnn.com/vault/article/magazine/MAG1066835/index.htm.

Laudeman, Tev. "A Freshman Helps Hire UK Coach, Then Plays for Him." *Echoes of Kentucky Basketball: The Greatest Stories Ever Told.* Ed. Scott Stricklin. Chicago: Triumph Books, 2006. 119-123.

Lindsey, Eric. "Cats Ride Hollywood Script into National Title Game." *UKathletics.com.* 5 April 2014. http://www.ukathletics.com/sports/m-baskbl/recaps/040514aaa.html.

Maloney, Mark. "Kentucky Baseball's Meyer Commands Attention in what Could Be His Final Start at Home." *The Lexington Herald-Leader.* 13 May 2011. http://www.kentucky.com/2011/05/13/1739207/kentucky-baseballs-meyer-commands.html.

Nelli, Bert. *The Winning Tradition: A History of Kentucky Wildcat Basketball*. Lexington: The University Press of Kentucky, 1984.

Pond, Dave. "Blue Blood." *Sharing the Victory Magazine*. March 2011. http://archives.fca.org/vsItemDisplay.1sp?.

Ramsey, Guy. "Where Are They Now: Cowgill Keeps Things in Perspective as He Waits for Call-Up." *UKathletics.com*. 7 July 2011. http://www.ukathletics.com/blog/2011/07/where-are-they-now.

Read, William F. "The Alltime Women's Team." *Sports Illustrated*. 10 Oct. 2007. http://sports illustrated.cnn.com/vault/article/magazine/MAG1115751/index.htm.

Rice, Russell. *Adolph Rupp: Kentucky's Basketball Baron*. Champaign, IL: Sagamore Publishing, 1994.

---. *The Wildcats: A Story of Kentucky Football*. Huntsville, AL: The Strode Publishers, Inc., 1975.

Rosales, Glen. "No Easy Task for Kentucky Women to Sink Hampton." *The Courier-Journal*. 18 March 2011. https://secure.pqarchiver.com/courier_journal/access/2297572321.html.

Royden, Norris. "Wildcats Come from Behind in Second Half to Beat Washington-Lee, 44-34." *Lexington Herald*. 5 Feb. 1926. http://www.bigbluehistory.net/bb/Statistics/Games/19260205WashingtonLee.html.

"Sean Woods." *gofrogs.com*. http://gofrogs.cstv.com/sports/m-baskbl/mtt/woods_sean00.html.

"Shipwreck Kelly." *Wikipedia, the free encyclopedia*. http://en.wikipedia.org/wiki/Shipwreck_Kelly.

Smith, Michael. "Even Cats Surprised They Thrashed Florida." *The Courier-Journal*. 6 Feb. 2003. https://secure.pqarchiver.com/courier_journal/access/1832511461.html.

---. "Kentucky 70, Florida 55; Showdown Blowdown." *The Courier-Journal*. 5 Feb. 2003. https://secure.pqarchiver.com/courier_journal/access/1832510611.html.

---. "Kentucky 106, Vanderbilt 44; UK Seniors Get Stylish Send-Off, Roll Past Vandy." *The Courier-Journal*. 6 March 2003. E1. https://secure.pqarchiver.com/courier_journal/access/1832531251.html.

---. "'Old School' Daniels." *The Courier-Journal*. 14 Feb. 2003. https://securepqarchiver.com/courier_journal/access/1832517071.html.

---. "Rondo Earns His Stripes." *The Courier-Journal*. 18 Dec. 2005. C1. https://secure.pqarchiver.com/courier_journal/access/1775151611.html.

---. "'Somebody Loves Us Up There.': Cats' Hail Mary Answered.": *The Courier-Journal*. 15 Jan. 2004. E1. https://secure/pqarchiver.com/courier_journal/access/1813332741.html.

---. "Wildcats Shoot Down No. 11 Volunteers, 80-78." *The Courier-Journal*. 2 March 2006. C1. https://secure.pqarchiver.com/courier_journal/access/1771844051.html.

Story, Mark. "The Reason to Stay True Blue." *Gr8ness: Celebrating the Kentucky Wildcats' 8th National Championship*. Lexington: Lexington Herald, Leader, 2012. 18-19.

Steinfort, Roy. "Rupp Chose Freshmen Over 2 Ex-All-Americans." *Louisville Courier-Herald*. 28 Feb. 1947. http://www.bigbluehistory.net.bb/dateline.html#allamericans.

Streble, James. "Kentucky Wildcats Football: Jojo Kemp Provides Hero Material." *ASea ofBlue.com*. 6 Oct. 2014. http://www.aseaofblue.com/2014/10/06/6918263/kentucky-wildcats-football-jojo-kemp-provides-hero-material;

Tipton, Jerry. "8th Wonders: Kentucky Wins 8th National Title, Beating Kansas 67-59." *Gr8ness: Celebrating the Kentucky Wildcats' 8th National Championship*. Lexington: Lexington Herald-Leader, 2012. 112, 115-17.

---. "Estill Steals Center Stage: Backup Big Man, Prince Boost Cats.": *Lexington Herald-Leader*. 18 March 2001. http://www.kentucky.com/2008/06/12/532407/estill-steals-center-stage.html.

---. "Fitch in Time Saves Bye: Clutch Three-Pointer Sends Cats to 70-67 Win." *Lexington Herald-Leader*. 3 March 2002. http://www.kentucky.com/2008/06/12/532437/fitch-in-time-saves-bye.html.

Trease, Denny. *Tales from the Kentucky Hardwood: A Collection of the Greatest Wildcat Basketball Stories Ever Told.* Champaign, IL: Sports Publishing L.L.C., 2002.

Tucker, Kyle. "Jojo Kemp Answers Call for Wildcats." *The Courier-Journal.* 2 Oct. 2014. http://www.courier-journal.com/story/sports/college/kentucky/2014/01/01-jojo-kemp-answers-call-kentucky-football-team/16563825/.

-----. "UK's Kickoff Team Savors Its Last Dance." *The Courier-Journal.* 9 Oct. 2014. http://www.courier-journal.com/story/college/kentucky/2014/10/09/kentucky-footballs-kickoff-team-savors-last-dance/16981141/.

Wahl. Grant. "He's the Shizz." *Sports Illustrated.* 11 Jan. 2010. http://sportsillustratd.cnn.com/vault/article/magazine/MAG1164564/index.htm.

White, Chris. "Kentucky Rifle Team Holds Off West Virginia to Win First NCAA Championship." *KentuckySports.com.* 13 March 2011. http://www.kentucky.com/2011/03/13/1668702/kentucky-rifle-team-holds-off.html.

Winn, Luke. "Fresh Start." *SI.com.* 7 April 2014. http://www.si.com/vault/2014/04/07/106450916/fresh-start.

Wolff, Alexander. "The Untouchables." *Sports Illustrated.* 8 April 1996. http://sportsillustrated.cnn.com/vault/article/magazine/MAG1007945/index.htm.

NAME INDEX
(LAST NAME, DEVOTION DAY NUMBER)

KENTUCKY

SCRIPTURES INDEX
(by DEVOTION DAY NUMBER)

208

WILDCATS